DARK LIGHT OF THE SOUL

DARK LIGHT OF THE SOUL

Kathryn Wood Madden

Kathryn Wood Madden

LINDISFARNE BOOKS
2008

2008
Lindisfarne Books
PO Box 749
Great Barrington, MA 01230
www.steinerbooks.org

Cover and book design: William Jens Jensen
Cover image by Alexandr Shebanov

Library of Congress Cataloging-in-Publication Data

Madden, Kathryn Wood.
  Dark light of the soul / Kathryn Wood Madden.
    p. cm.
  Includes bibliographical references (p. 257).
  ISBN 978-1-58420-065-9
  1. Psychology, Religious. 2. Psychology and religion.
  3. Experience (Religion) 4. Jung, C. G. (Carl Gustav), 1875–1961.
  5. Böhme, Jakob, 1575–1624. 6. Mysticism. I. Title.
  BL53.M3615 2008
  200.1'9—dc22
                                                    2008040892

Contents

Acknowledgments

Barry Ulanov said once to me that one of the greatest gifts we can offer another person is that of a supportive presence. I would like to acknowledge the many persons who have given me such during the writing of this book.

I would like to thank my patients who, while their names and partial identities have been changed to respect their anonymity, I am very grateful for their allowing me to tell their stories. Without them, I would have only what one patient calls "a castle surrounded by clouds and air with no foundation." The persons who have shared their struggles, dreams, and visions in this text are the ground and flesh of this endeavor.

The warm encouragement of my therapist colleagues in New York, Don Kalsched, Carol Fox, Joan Kavanaugh, my friend Terah Cox, Bonnie Ward, and Bette Hack consistently have given me the supportive entry to my own experience of the unconscious, the encouragement to take risks, to dig deeper, and to move into the abyss itself, confident that there would always be the intervention of an angel.

Ewert Cousins, Professor of Theology Emeritus at Fordham University, Randall Styers, Associate Professor of Philosophy at the University of North Carolina, and Harry Fogarty, lecturer at Union Theological Seminary and Jungian analyst have inspired my work and the choice of my sources. They have challenged me to see further to the more complex fact of the opposites of opposites.

Ann Ulanov, along with her husband Barry, represent the beginning and end of this piece. They have been the living reality of the central image of my work. In their reciprocity of being, I have learned the deeper meaning of exchange.

Much of this work is about interrelationship and the importance of otherness on many levels. Each of us is inexorably linked to the other. In the writing of this piece, I have emphasized that a person's developmental reality is only one level of experience. Yet, the gift of loving parents also can assist in enabling us to "see through" to a larger truth. Even though they are gone from this world, I would like to acknowledge my parents, Doris and Fergus Wood.

Finally, there is my husband, Ron. That other half who is at the intersection of one's soul, contributes to the *temenos*, the sacred space in which reflection and growth can occur that allows for the Self to unfold. The Self of one includes the other because the Self contains a profound circumference. In essence, this journey has been as transformational for Ron as it has for me. As von Franz says, it becomes difficult to tell at some point who is mirroring whom. For this lovely man, who has the gift of groundedness, intelligence, and laughter, and, most important, recognition of "the deep," I am forever grateful.

PREFACE

IN AN AGE focused increasingly upon a cultural, political, and social understanding of otherness as diversity, preferring to ponder God, if at all, mostly in terms of *immanence*, depth psychology is in danger of becoming *breadth* psychology. The search for transcendence has become more and more the province of New Age weekend workshops. On the other hand, depth psychology that seeks only the transpersonal without the incarnate spirit in the flesh of everyday relationships in history may likewise prove to be a failed enterprise.

In such an era, we may expand our vision to reviewing something of the inner journeys of the seventeenth-century Protestant mystic Jacob Boehme and the twentieth-century depth psychologist C. G. Jung. Each was passionately engaged with the immediacy of experience, yet each believed in the vital importance of spirit as a real and transforming presence in human life. Reflection upon the crosscurrents in the experiences and select writings of these two intriguing visionaries may help to ground the work that we do as depth psychologists, clinical practitioners, teachers, and those whose interests lie in the arenas of religious experience and spirituality.

In this work, I compare and contrast Boehme's and Jung's experiences with a special focus on the religious or psychological experience of what Erich Neumann calls *unitary reality*, a ground of being that contains all opposites in potentiality. I examine and analyze these experiences from the overlapping yet distinct viewpoints of depth psychology and religion, with the goal of offering what I find meaningful for anyone who is on the journey of healing and wholeness—as well as instructive to the professional working in a clinical setting.

I

UNITARY REALITY

THIS BOOK RESTS on the premise that a unitary reality underlies all psychological experience. The experience of this unitary reality is the culmination of an encounter with the deepest layer of the collective unconscious, the psychoid, archetypal layer, in which we meet all forms of otherness. The otherness we meet at this depth of experience is so radically transforming that all that was formerly known to us and thought to be real from the ego's point of view is surpassed. Drawing from Jacob Boehme's and Carl Jung's images of radical otherness, a new reality is born—the Self in Jung's terms, Christ in Boehme's terms—a unitary reality that enables us to see through our newly constellated reality to our former origins, to a pre-differentiated, universal ground.

Innate to this experience of depth, we find throughout history and in comparative literature that, psychologically speaking, a breakdown of varying degrees often accompanies a breakthrough to this unitary reality. Deintegration, or fragmentation, seem to be important aspects preceding the integration of all the disparate parts that are contained in what is experienced psychologically as unitary reality, or oneness. The experience of unitary reality may be a single event that happens once as a way for the personality to restructure and locate a new intrapsychic core from which the ego can proceed in its development. More often, unitary reality is the culmination of a long process of struggle and suffering that we engage in through analysis or psychotherapy or spiritual direction, or even through our own creative endeavors of seeking, in which we are led down, or *in*to the Black Hole of what Martin Buber called "the divine Void."

Jungian analyst Erich Neumann, who analyzed with Jung and practiced as an analyst in Tel Aviv, describes this breakthrough event or process as "a borderline experience of the beginning of all things that corresponds to the mystic's experience of the universal diffusion of the unitary reality" (Neumann, 1989, p.74).

The outcome of the experience of unitary reality is a meeting of human spirit with divine spirit. This conjunction or sacred marriage conjoins the spirit of the divine with the body of nature. Our consciousness changes. We begin to know that we have a distinct and personal identity that is known by something far more vast and more transpersonal than our ego. We are infused with new confidence that this other that knows us so distinctly will embrace the specificity of our identity long after the ego and the body that houses it have passed back into the earth. Thus, the process of struggle and becoming very attentive to our inner lives, images, and feelings is a worthwhile endeavor since it gives meaning to existence.

Becoming active participants in the vital process of life-transforming encounter with the collective unconscious requires that we attend not only to the role of experience but to the fact of purposive suffering, suffering in this case pertaining not to masochism but to wrestling with the opposites of psychological material. When we engage with the opposites within us, of our projective tendencies and our projective identifications, the ego inevitably suffers. It is no longer the center of psychological life, and this is painful, especially initially.

The experience of unitary reality, or knowledge of it, makes a difference in clinical work and the study of analytical psychology because unitary reality contains all diversity, all otherness, both in terms of experience and of persons. Analytically, we get glimpses of unitary reality in the radical otherness of dreams, in the transference and countertransference, through the experience of the transcendent function, and in and through the trauma of breakdown, creative depression, deintegration experience, or what Jungian analyst John Weir-Perry refers to as *spiritual emergency* or acute episodes.

These experiences that lead us to the knowledge of unitary reality have relevance to clinical practice because they are so transforming. As we work with the imagination, our emotions, images, and dreams suffering, we grow and change. Sometimes, we achieve potential that we never could have imagined was part of our personal blueprint. Whether the transformation that begins to occur leads to healing or to dissolution is of great concern to the practitioner. It is not that we should fear dissolution in a containing context, but there are specific things that the analyst needs to watch for in terms of the ego becoming totally overwhelmed, inflated, or deflated into a clinical depression. In later chapters, I will give examples of how the analyst can discern what road the patient is on (and what to do about it).

I have chosen the two central figures of Jacob Boehme and Carl Jung as my initial examples of the experience of unitary reality because they engaged so deeply with the collective unconscious, suffered profoundly, and brought back knowledge that has given us a window into the depth of experience to which I wish to attest.

In offering them as illustrations, I will compare their primary images of unitary reality—the *Ungrund* and the Pleroma—and focus upon the *nature* of the experience itself. Boehme and Jung use different vocabularies that I also will compare and contrast while emphasizing depth psychological concepts that house their common experience.

A secondary theme is threaded throughout the text, namely, depth psychology can make a valuable contribution to the contemporary conversation on diversity and otherness.

Diversity refers to the distinctions we recognize in gender, race, ethnicity, and lifestyle choices. Otherness refers to the ego's view of any of a variety of inner psychological contents including, but not limited to, the relational level of otherness, the primordial level of otherness, and the level or layer of otherness radical enough to be perhaps conceived of as unbound, although connected to, the ego and the psyche—spirit. Depth psychology is uniquely positioned to explore all these layers.

The relational level is important in terms of our exploring projection and introjection, not only to others but also to other people's otherness (difference) from us. Depth psychology certainly is able to work with the level of projection and introjection, but further, to probe beyond developmental issues and to explore the frontiers of otherness at the primordial level of the psyche. By primordial, I am referring to that of the psyche that exists at the beginning of time (L. *"primus,"* first, *"ordiri,"* begin).

At the primordial level, depth psychology raises to consciousness a new experience of otherness, a *transcendent ultimacy* beyond the psyche that continuously encroaches upon, seduces, dismembers, and transforms surface immediacy. *Surface immediacy* pertains to our experience of the real at the level of our needs and projections.

Transcendent ultimacy, in contrast, pertains to experience in which our previous notions and images of God, the transcendent, the ultimate—whatever we call it—are shattered and redefined through this experience I am calling a *unitary reality.* The *abyss* of spirit may be so other that it feels as if it is beyond our categories of understanding altogether. This presence may render us speechless. Or, if we can speak and describe, we might claim that the quality of this otherness, this Holy Other, is a "Wholly Other," beyond being itself, even beyond God and our conceptions of God.

Because so much tension exists in the world in the way each of us apprehends the divine, we sorely need a way of working with our psyches; this is imperative, in fact, to human existence and survival in the face of terrorism, fundamentalism, and archetypal evil. We need to locate and work within a psycho-spiritual umbrella that is large enough to house contradictions. Within the archetypal realm of the psyche, there is most definitely potential to order the opposites of diverse experience without eliminating the essence of what makes our neighbor other.

In order to expand our psychological comprehension of otherness, we need to build the intrapsychic muscles necessary for embracing tension, contradiction, and paradox. Learning to house tension and to hold the polarities of otherness are central to exploring the nature of the transcendent, how it might function creatively within the realm of human relatedness. It is within the embrace of contraries, the "yes" and the "no" of life needing each other, that we might find new ways to strive toward a restorative, healing peace in ourselves and in the world, even in the face of overwhelming evidence to the contrary.

I have chosen Jung and Boehme as relevant figures to illustrate the above notions because they have experienced the abyss and have returned to tell of it. Not everyone does. They have fostered new categories of experience, giving us a fresh and accessible understanding of how the transcendent moves among us. They have an immediate grasp of consciousness as psychological process, and they proceed with psychological insight that arguably takes place in spirit. By spirit, I refer to something actual and real, as do my sources. We discover the nature of spiritual freedom within the dialectic of opposites in the psyche.

Jung focuses upon an immediate relation to transforming spirit. For Jung the qualities of spirit are present to ground or inform the psychoanalytic encounter between patient and analyst, conscious and unconscious. Spirit is significant in the clinical setting in its tendency to fuel both complexes and healing.

Jung's relevance to a discourse between religion and depth psychology is that the psyche *is* the medium through which we apprehend and keep alive an existential grasp of the presence of the transcendent. This presence is experienced by the psyche in the form of an archetype, particularly the Self archetype, a psychic center linked to instinct and characterized by the features of numinosity, autonomy, and unconsciousness. Ultimately, his approach to spirit is as an archetype, and also a reality transcending the ego and the contents of the objective psyche. In general, an archetype is expressed by a symbol that is a captivating, although enigmatic, portrayal of archetypal reality itself, often leading us toward a reorientation of our conscious position.

For Jung, attending to symbolic process means that the ego must relate to the unconscious contents of the psyche that are often represented in dreams or waking fantasies of opposition, contrasexual otherness, or cast-off otherness. As we correspond with these inner contents through a deliberate exercise of reflection, whether in analysis, therapy, spiritual direction, or other forms that allow for a depth of reflection, eventually a third factor or position emerges through what Jung calls the transcendent function of the psyche. When the transcendent function is activated, a symbol begins to unfold in pictorial, tactile, or auditory statements and images that represent a synthesis of the opposing elements and a resolution to the conscious conflict (Jung, 1921, par. 825; Jung's *Collected Works* are cited by publication date and paragraph). The transcendent function of the psyche is a crucial conduit of perception through which unitary reality is experienced.

Attending to this conscious-unconscious process fuels a living, symbolic process: one vivid, alive, inspiring, meaningful, wherein we begin to understand the specific significance of our individual symbols that, simultaneously, point toward, and participate in, their archetypal source *and* its own source. When we begin to pay attention to this innate capacity, our lives change significantly as we develop the inner psychological strength to deal with the opposites and with paradox that we often rationalize out of experience or ignore because it is painful or provokes anxiety.

Being of religious roots and unknowledgeable of depth psychology in the seventeenth century, Boehme thinks of spirit as the kindling, animating power, or soul of existence. For him, spirit emanates not only from God, but significantly also from a primal preexistent freedom that is before God. Boehme's apprehension of spirit is another sort of reality altogether, a certainty that he attests to that gives meaning to existence rather than being merely a layer or part of existence. In *Three Principles of the Divine Essence*, Boehme speaks of how he understands the structure of divine-human relationship. As summarized by scholar Arthur Versluis, Boehme says,

> God the Father is the First Principle, the Divine Essence; the Second Principle is the Holy Spirit, associated with the "Light-World"; and between these two is the Third Principle, which includes the elemental and sidereal world, where the counterposed powers of Satan and Christ appear (Versluis, 1999, pp. 13–15).

Versluis goes on to explain that Boehme's Second Principle (that of spirit) is "opened unto us" by "living in the Third Principle." We could say that there are correlations between Boehme's Third Principle, with its "counterposed powers," and Jung's "world of opposites." Further, Boehme's Second Principle (of spirit), which is "opened unto us" as we wrestle with the counterposed powers, appears to be analogous to Jung's transcendent function that leads us to an experience of the Self, the archetype that contains all opposites.

But, for Boehme, more than a principle, spirit is direct immediate experience. He grasps this immediacy in the way he gets inside himself and is honest about what is passing through his consciousness. He does not deny what exists but claims it with visceral honesty, intuiting and acknowledging both the transcendent and the immanent as intrinsic to the expression of spirit in terms of unitary reality. Spirit, as it inspires (*inspirare*: to breathe) the inward union of two beings, breathes the essence of soul from one into the "other" and thus imprints the other with what Boehme calls its *signature*.

The activity of spirit in Boehme and Jung, which is so present and vital, expands our notions of human freedom. Our conception of what it means to be in relationship with an other is expanded considerably beyond categories of "other" determined by the ego that are bound by the intrapsychic and/or externalized products of introjection and projection.

For Jung, the other is any part different from the ego with which we are identified. Jung's notion of individuation centers upon the development of personality, which is a practical and inevitable process for all of us throughout our lives; but he further emphasizes the profound creativity, and the possibility of rather profound healing and transformation that is possible when the opposites of otherness in the psyche are confronted consciously. As the ego (necessary to us, but actually not the center, or central force of psychological structure) opens to and can relate to the otherness intrinsic to the nature of the human psyche, the ego is thereby relativized but not annihilated.

The individuation process in its fulfillment is called by Jung the *coniunctio oppositorum* or the union of opposites that embraces and reconciles all contraries (noting that there are various levels of *oppositorum*). Jung's immediate way of knowing gives us a valuable method for knowing how these expressions of contrariness, as they occur in and through the psyche, can be identified, related to, and synthesized. Our inner house gets stretched and we begin to understand the scriptural essences of the notion of "many mansions." Not only does life become increasingly interesting as a result of this inner expansiveness, but also things begin to come to us that we never would have expected, because the ego is no longer holding us captive to restrictive projections.

And then there is Jung's idea of *unus mundus*, the conception of a unitary world based upon a principle of acausality, which has bearing in this discussion. Currently, this concept of *unus mundus* is being considered in terms of an interactive field in analysis (*cf.* Schwartz-Salant, 1995, p. 2). The *unus mundus* is a unitary world (psychologically speaking) that offers glimpses of a unitary reality while, at the same time, emphasizing the relations existing between things and the relations between relations. Each stratum of existence is understood to be linked with all other strata in this original unity. So, we have the experience of the whole but also that of the parts of the whole. Not only is this experience awe-inspiring, it also aligns us with external otherness in a way that is crucial to our global identity as we strive toward a global consciousness in which we do not need to obliterate one another.

[handwritten marginal note: "Many mansions"]

[handwritten marginal note: "because"]

Jung speaks of the *unus mundus* as connected to the archetype as psychoid. *Psychoid* for him suggests that psyche and matter may be two aspects of one and the same thing (Jung, 1960, par. 418). In other words, the archetype may be capable of manifesting in both material and psychical forms of existence (Ibid., pars. 840–841), meaning that what we glimpse as otherness in the psychoid event is a linking of the psychic and material worlds. These events do not coincide in time and space, but they do occasionally intersect physical and psychic reality and give us the background for discerning psychological meaning.

Unlike the more fundamental levels of the unconscious that I have mentioned, the psychoid level is not easily accessible to consciousness; but, when intersected, it gives us glimpses of a unitary reality. My purpose in offering the examples of Boehme and Jung's experience of the abyss/ *Ungrund* and Pleroma as other is to illustrate this layer of unconscious activity.

Clinically, the therapeutic value of the other in the process of individuation leads toward the healing experience of a unitary reality in which analyst and patient may be directed by an actual event or process to areas of traumatization or suffering that otherwise remain unconscious. Boehme and Jung offer valuable examples that exemplify processes and psychological events that are helpful to our understanding similar occurrences in the clinical transference, in dreams, and through the synthesizing effect of the transcendent function.

The process and/or event of unitary reality is a healing one. It is healing in that at the level of the archetypal as psychoid we also glimpse the reality of the Self, what Jung calls the archetype of the center. The Self mediates for the individual both poles of the archetype and bridges between material and psychical forms of existence. The experience of the Self is of having spirit *in* the body. The patient may begin to experience having a center, even though this internal kernel of core-self is initially experienced as other and continues to have its own independent life even after the ego comes to consciousness of it.

The Self opens us to the experience of all-encompassing worldliness. We exist anew with the perception that there is unity in all things even though this perception may be for only fifteen minutes, as we shall see with one of Boehme's experiences, or for flashes here and there, clinically, when the analyst carries one of the poles of the patient's psyche for a time before the patient can relate to it and integrate it consciously.

As the manifestation of Self is constellated, we usually feel very alive, hooked by an impetus of desire that pulls us forward like a great magnet, and we often feel the polarities of life-death, joy-sorrow, light-dark, safety-paranoia, moral imposition-ego justification—many opposites—oscillating back and forth in us as the Self makes its presence known. Simultaneously, the ego is thrown off-base and loses its position of central command. We can become terribly confused and fearful, a fear that is impending and ominous, life-threatening, at least as the ego perceives it.

If we move away from the center the Self has forged with its penetrating otherness, depending upon what this central archetype has in store for us in terms of what in us needs integrating, we may feel anything from terror to bliss, or both, as opposite positions emerge through an internal dialogue, completely throwing off what we thought we knew. We are presented with the tremendous challenge of hanging on for the duration of what may last for minutes or days, months, or years. At best, if we can hold the center, converse with it, translate its contents into life, then we most often can feel the abundant flow of creativity, new ideas, new forms of expression as spirit surges into our life directing and redirecting our activity.

Later chapters devoted to clinical examples will give us raw and contemporary material to explore the Self event and process at the psychoid level, which Jung also refers to as the somatic unconscious (1988, pp. 44,1ff.). In contrast to the psychic unconscious, which is for Jung more about our psychological movement on a mental-spiritual level in which images, patterns, and causality are the informing materials of individuation, the (psychoid) somatic unconscious is more about a psycho-physical layer of reality. What is efficacious for the healing and wholeness of some persons may be less about the *prima materia* of mental and spiritual processes and more about the restoration of spirit in the body, in matter.

In instances of severe trauma, Jung's concept of the archetype as psychoid alerts us to a revolutionary notion, one in which the unfolding of the Self as an innate and potential bridging reality links the material and psychical, inner and outer, in one reality. We may go in and out of this reality, but once we know it is there and that it is real, it makes a difference. For instance, we might realize that our childhood injuries are not entirely dependent upon our mother or father's reality but instead upon unitary reality, a oneness that is present to us beyond our first caregivers.

I am emphasizing the possibility for healing, even for those with more severe trauma, by working in relationship with another person toward a meeting of human and divine spirit. Over time, as the presence of remembered oneness is allowed authentically in the relationship, we begin to live into and to integrate *into* our conscious experience the potential unity of all opposites that we once experienced in a pre-differentiated state of being. This pre-differentiated state of being reaches all the way back in time, to the mother of our developmental years, and before time, to that moment of severance from our creator, the moment in which we became incarnate.

Unitary reality, and all the trials and suffering that are entailed in forging a relationship with this reality, gives us hope beyond hope that there is a preexistent ground of unitary reality. This preexistent ground exists, is personal, knows us, and we can relate to it in a meaningful way through tools of the psyche that we inherit. Knowing and experiencing this reality, even once, can sustain our restless souls for a lifetime with an inspired confidence that only the ego and body will die—there is something more eternal at this primal center that transcends death and sustains aliveness in some form that we cannot claim to know yet.

Crucially, given this point of view, an individual's potential for wholeness would not be entirely dependent upon a human being—the maternal figure so emphasized in most psychoanalytic developmental theory—who is a limited human being like all the rest of us. Our impetus in psychological work would be reclaiming one's birthright to live in the image of our original ground.

Jung, for one, claims that the physical and psychic are possibly but two aspects of one and the same underlying reality. The world of matter, then, is a mirror-image of the world of spirit or of the psyche, and vice versa (Jung, 1963, pars. 766–69). Quantum physics is confirming this notion of mirror image. An image of this "vice versa" might be that of a great universal conjunction of all that is vital of nature with all that is alive of spirit. The idea would be the possibility of consummating a relationship to this larger Self that bridges heaven and earth as a creative act penultimate only to heaven itself.

Clinically, to access later in an adult life what is stored or hidden at this difficult and fairly inaccessible psychoid and somatic layer, we would have to access not only what is unconscious in the usual psychic sense—for example, with the images and emotions we know and are familiar with—but also the somatic, or body-matter, pole that is so unconscious that it feels to be unconscious to the unconscious itself. In other words, what is known even at the primordial level has to be encountered and relinquished as known to meet what is beyond it, more unconscious, more unknown. In essence, it means encountering what is totally unknown from the conscious viewpoint of the ego, and it involves the body specifically.

The nature of the trauma is "doubly *un-conscious*" given the fact that the psychoid-and-somatic level of reality is already tremendously inaccessible. Our usual, causal measures of accessing trauma at the level of the psychic unconscious (mental images) would therefore not be particularly mutative.

What would be the nature of the experience necessary to access this psychoid layer? What would the experience feel like? How would we access and approach such states of unknowing in a way that promotes healing and circulation to this very difficult and impenetrable layer?

Boehme and Jung give witness to this layer of existence. The Pleroma for Jung and the *Ungrund* for Boehme grounded the fact of a unitary reality for both, a "window to eternity," which enabled them to see through their newly constellated realities (the Self, and Christ) to a pre-differentiated, universal ground.

For Boehme, there are similar layers of otherness to Jung's. Otherness for him takes on a more spiritual language. Analogous to the projection and introjection level of surface immediacy in Jung, otherness for Boehme pertains to the outward life. The outward life can border dangerously upon becoming an external shell when it becomes one-sidedly rational and devoid of deep feeling. Otherness at this level pertains to our being subject to worldly spirit in contrast to the immediacy of divine spirit.

At the primordial level, which points beyond the psyche but still is of the psyche, Boehme speaks of otherness as the fact of wrath and evil thrust directly into the fact of silent emptiness and the good. He insists that the imagination connects us to the center of existence while distinguishing imagination from a fantasy that separates us from reality (1978, p. 103). At the deepest center of imagination, "What remains hidden since the beginning of the world" becomes a mystery that we can apprehend and hold in our consciousness.

Here, like Jung, Boehme attests to another level of radically other otherness. The realm outside of time and space is accessible and real. Boehme attests that experience of the divine is beyond any of our rational categories and can best be described as a void or an abyss. What psychology speculates is an interactive field may be analogous to Boehme's experience of the *Ungrund* as a negative presence that is full. He is referring to something beyond the ego, beyond the unconscious, to the divine, although he tends to equate the divine with the unconscious. Nonetheless, what he is referring to is a movement of the ego to something positive, real, and transformative.

Methodologically, in lining up the images of the radical otherness—*Ungrund* and Pleroma for Boehme and Jung—I will briefly discuss the different vocabularies of the two in the context of spirit and otherness. Additionally, I will address some of the resistances to otherness at this level of experience that are evident not only in individuals, but also on a cultural level. My primary focus will be to elucidate notions drawn from their individual experience that are applicable to the healing of persons in clinical practice.

Boehme and Jung, in their respective ways, are open to participating in the immediacy of transforming spirit. They share an interest in the world of the subject and a concern for the interior life.

Although they meet in these specific ways, there are also some differences between them that distinguish them as theologian and as depth psychologist. There remains, for Boehme, a seventeenth-century German man, something ineffable in religious experience. At the other end of the spectrum, Jung, a twentieth-century man of Swiss descent, focuses upon manifestations in the clinical encounter, often skipping over the subject of another layer of existence beyond the objective unconscious altogether. He does talk, however, about God beyond the objective psyche and thinks we do have a soul that is "related to deity," which we are capable of knowing.

In the examples of Boehme and Jung, we see that unitary reality underlies all psychological experience. In the encounter of both men with the deepest layer of the collective unconscious, they meet all forms of otherness including radically other otherness. What was known to be real from the ego's perspective is surpassed. A star is born—a unitary reality that enables them to see through the psyche to a pre-differentiated, universal ground.

2

Distinctions between
Psychology and Religion

On the subject of experience, the boundaries between psychology and religion are humanly forged but the *Anton Boison* membrane between them is a permeable one. Clearly religion and depth psychology share a mutual interest in the world of primordial experience. Both participate in a concern for the nurture and sustenance of interior life. They do so differently.

At the center of the depth-psychological encounter is the psyche and the immediacy of our experience of it and through it. At the center of the theological inquiry is the mystery of the transcendent and our experience of it. The challenge is to maintain the individual integrity of each discipline and link them in conversation. When we begin to allow some form of communication between psychological and theological sources of method to relate experience and what transcends it, we are asking how psychological process affects religious experience and how the transcendent functions in the psyche.

METHODOLOGICAL TENSIONS

Religion preserves the view that there remains something ineffable in human experience that seems often to elude the grasp of psychology. Depth psychology too easily falls into the snares of psychologism since it is, by nature, empirical (the claim that knowledge is limited to sensory experience or observation), and phenomenological (a method based on a reflective and descriptive study of consciousness that concentrates on the objects of direct experience but not the nature of being). Jung, for instance, often skipped over the subject of metaphysics altogether, although he sometimes borrows theological language or makes direct translation of theology into psychology to explain what he discovered in the psyche.

Religion can be defensive in keeping established religious facts distinct from hypotheses about these facts, claiming that where metaphysics is involved, religious interpretation is called for with its own language and procedures. For example, many religions ground themselves on revelation. Employing a phenomenological approach to revelation can be dangerous. As Paul Ricœur says, phenomenology begins with reduction. It "begins by a humiliation or wounding of the knowledge belonging to immediate consciousness" (Ricœur, 1970, p. 377).

At the same time, religion can step over into the domain of psychology when it imposes religious motives and values upon transference alliance, the relationship that forms between analyst and patient, and presses intentionally toward a "spiritual communion in which both (persons) rely upon God" (Tournier, 1954, pp. 12–21). If an analyst ignores the patient's own frame of reference and instead resorts to an agenda of proclamation, what is promoted as a theology of grace may be as detrimental to the analytic process as psychologistic immanentism is. In cases where an analyst believes his/her endeavor to be one of salvation, then the inflation of the countertransference may diminish the distinctions of the two separate fields and compromise the integrity of the psyche through an inability to remain neutral.

A method that preserves the integrity of each discipline yet also explores some of the material common to both psychology and religion at the depths of the human psyche seems to be more expansive.

METHOD OF EXCHANGE

The method I propose is one of exchange. I will examine the experience of Boehme and Jung by looking for the synthesizing third. Where Boehme and Jung intersect is in the act of meeting the primordial and numinous at great levels of depth in the psyche. They meet the opposites of the psyche within themselves as these opposites exist. They record their experiences and they interpret their experiences. Both actively embrace the fact of suffering and yet continue to respond to what they find in relation to spirit as I have defined it at the level of radical otherness. The most significant element shared by them is the fact of an inherent transcending principle: for Jung, the Self; for Boehme, Christ and Divine Wisdom. This third bridging factor integrates the opposites at a different level and provides the basis for a valid comparison between them. To ground the fact and existence of this transcending principle in the psyche, as Jung does, is important, but, I believe, incomplete. Thus:

1. At one level of comparison, my method explores the transcendent experienced immediately in the individual psyches of Boehme and Jung.
2. On another level of comparison, my method places the experience of the two in an exchange.
3. On a third level of comparison, my method evokes my own response in relation to their opposites as these opposites intersect in me. Thus, my method is more than just an exchange of views. In other words, spirit underlies even the datum of the material.
4. Finally, I will explore by method of comparison how the transcendent exists as a process in clinical work as gathered through the data of immediate experience in the consulting room.

Recalling that unitary reality underlies the entire psychological process, I believe that Boehme and Jung vividly attest to this fact in their grasp of what is. For both Boehme and Jung, the primordial is real, but it is spirit that conjoins the concrete with the universal. We meet spirit through the activity of our deeper self as we penetrate and are penetrated by that transcendent factor in us that is dynamic and free.

As the synthesizing third, the transcendent function occurs clinically: another layer of reality at times becomes evident in the exchange. This layer of reality moves us beyond self-referential categories altogether and leads us into an area that is less easy to describe. Beyond what we know, as philosopher Donald Wood notes, we receive glimpses of "conscious communion or participation in a timeless reality" (Wood, 1982, p. 209).

Here, the actuality of time is not eliminated but we feel temporarily outside it. Eternity, however momentary, feels to be no longer like an abstract heaven but as if one were part and parcel with the stars.

The unconscious, as we come to know it at this level of exchange, impinges upon a form of existence outside time and space (Wood, p. 209). The idea of a "completed individuation" (cf. Jung, 1963, p. 296) straddles psychological experience and preternatural experience.

The eternal for Jung, Boehme, and for many of the authors I draw from in support of unitary reality, is a transcendent a priori reality that is in motion, moving toward us, shattering our consciousness, summoning us with intense desire if we are willing to probe beyond our psychological independence to receive what is archetypally present and spiritually actual.

More than a stasis, something counterpoised and in-and-of-itself, spirit meets us as a dynamic reality at the abyss level, at the level of radical otherness, and points beyond itself. As we are receptive to spirit, the veil that has previously obscured our view lifts. Mystical communion is real and is not limited to saints and mystics.

EXPERIENCE AS A WAY OF KNOWING

Then I saw that on the shaft there hung a human figure that held within itself all the loneliness of the world and of the spaces. Alone, and hoping for nothing, the One hung and gazed down into the void. For long the One gazed, drawing all solitude unto itself. Then deep in the fathomless dark was born an infinitesimal spark. Slowly it rose from the bottomless depth, and as it rose it grew until it became a star. And the star hung in space just opposite the figure, and the white light streamed upon the Lonely One. (Wickes, 1950, p. 245)

A method of exchange emerges from a specific way of knowing in which we can live in relation to this eternity of unitary reality. We have an incredible means of relating to the symbol and to our inner life through our primordial or religious experience. Jung presents the above testimony of individuation symbolism drawing from a patient of Frances Wickes, a psychoanalyst greatly influenced by the psychology of Jung, as an example of the birth of the imagination (cf. Jung, 1959b, 344n). Similarly, my focus is on experience that incarnates, which breaks in on us through the unconscious in dreams and imagination, which informs us in an *inner way*. I have referred to this as experience that transforms our surface immediacy, or as something that persistently breaks into ordinary events of our lives and seizes us.

I am interested in inner experience that leads into dimensions of the unconscious that point beyond us. As Antoine Faivre, Professor of Religious Studies at the Sorbonne, says,

> What is important here is not what is consciously presented to individuals, but only what so extends *the human consciousness that human existence with all its light and dark sides can be affirmed and shaped*, and the meaningfulness of life can be *experienced* [italics mine]. (1995, p. 385)

The experience of the Self in Jung's terms, the experience and what Boehme calls the realization of Christ, finds some common ground in naming reality. A method that embraces reality is specific to the clinical practice of depth psychology, but at many levels equally applicable to any discipline that engages with the psychology of the unconscious, inclusive of its contents.

Further, my method and approach center upon the belief that our inner experience in some way prefigures something else. As we relate to the primordial or archetypal images and symbols that we encounter, we are given markers that stake a perimeter that encircles a central vision. The vision itself is boundless. If we keep these markers constantly in view, albeit their sometimes contrary natures, we proceed toward an inner way that has to do with the maturing of the self in psychological terms, the soul in terms of religion. This Self is affirmed in the analytic tradition as individuation and in the Christian tradition as the soul's immediate experience of divine spirit. Other traditions and disciplines—from art to literature to philosophy—equally have access to the potentially arresting new birth that resonates with primordial experience (cf. Ulanov, B., 1992, for instance).

IMAGES AND CONTRASTS

As I have said, this approach is distinguished by its interiority. *Interiority* refers to the process of engaging our images and numinous experiences *from the inside view*. We are attending to our images and contrasts from the inside out as these are reflected or echoed back to us from the larger magnetic, or archetypal field.

I am making the distinction, which I will continue to expand upon, that what we usually mean by image (as in "image of God") is related to a positive or direct representation of something. Much of our religious experience is of this positive nature, as in kataphatic theology. As Ewert

Cousins, Professor of Theology Emeritus at Fordham University, writes,

> the phrase "image of God" contains two positive affirmations: it identifies the human person as an image and, without any qualifications makes a straightforward affirmation of God. (1990, p. 59)

This statement describes one way we experience God in which God is "grasped in his positive perfection" and "this absolute, as positive perfection, is reflected in the image." Implicit in this form of consciousness is a "differentiated self" (Ibid., p. 67). By *differentiation*, Cousins means that in this form of religious experience, the soul remains of a separate essence ontologically and psychologically. "The metaphysical content of the divine reality is present in a positive or kataphatic fashion" but the self "does not necessarily touch the ontologically divine" (Ibid., p. 67).

The expression of kataphatic experience as positive is distinctly different from the "what is not" experience of apophatic theology. Cousins asks us to consider "the experience of God as the real," as not only one that reflects the light of God in the sense of reflecting the image of a mirror (speculum) (Ibid., p. 64), but also one that is "beyond the persons of the Trinity," beyond the positive attributes and determinations of God and is instead a venture "into the divine abyss, the naked absolute" (Ibid., p. 69).

"Does the soul remain in an image of God in that experience?" Cousins asks. "Yes" he answers, "but in a way that seems to erase its very status" (Ibid., p. 69), meaning that "all ontological and psychological grounds of even a divinely imaged self seem to disappear" (Ibid., p. 69). How does this happen? A part of the self, which Cousins calls the "abyss of the self plunges into the divine abyss, or better, finds itself undifferentiated from the divine abyss. There in that divine abyss questions of differentiation cannot arise" (Ibid., p. 69).

Cousins finds both of these forms of experience—fullness and/or emptiness—to be valid and mutually affirming. In fact, as he suggests, they may be "compatible even within the same person" (Ibid., p. 69).

At what layer of human experience would we find the "abyss of the self"? Does abyss of the self have something to do with Jung's psychoid layer and with Boehme's experience of the *Ungrund?* Does the divine abyss of undifferentiated reality point to a reality beyond it, perhaps a pre-differentiated form of the soul? How does depth psychology approach such a rich understanding of an inside view that is inclusive of both images?

Following Cousins, I suggest an analogy that may be helpful and that may lead toward a more expansive view of how we understand through primordial and religious experience what it might mean to be in the image drawing from levels of experience other than the kataphatic, or positive. To use the mirror image, truly, a mirror usually reflects, so living in the image and reflecting God's "interpenetrating light, like light shining in a mirror" (Ibid., p. 65) is certainly one way that an individual brings to reflective awareness the image of God.

Interestingly, mirrors are both plane or spherical. Spherical mirrors are small portions of the surface of a sphere.

A sphere is defined in geometry as a ball or globe bounded by a surface that is everywhere equally

distant from a central point. Any geometric
sectioning of a hollow sphere by a plane will be a
circle; when the plane passes through the center of
the sphere, the resulting section is a great circle; any
other section is a small circle. A straight line from
the center to the surface is a radius. (*Encyclopedia
Americana*, 1959, p. 402)

A mirror that is spherical has properties, at least in small
portion, of the surface of a sphere. The surface of a sphere,
even sectioned or cut in half as a spherical mirror would be,
as it is intersected by any plane maintains the properties of
a circle. What intersects it and forms a section (see opposite) has the properties of a small circle.

At any point, the surface of the sphere may be intersected by a plane, and the surface is everywhere equally
distant from a central point. A sphere is visually both center
and circumference, but bear in mind that to have the properties of the greater sphere, the plane "passes through the
center" and, in so doing, has also the identical properties
of what it intersects. Thinking back on Cousin's notion of
the abyss of the self plunging into the divine abyss and finding itself undifferentiated from it, let us look at a spherical
mirror that has the same attributes as a sphere, although
serving the purpose of mirroring.

In a spherical mirror, concave or convex, the line
through the center of the spherical surface of which
the mirror is a part and the middle point of the mirror is called "the axis." From a concave mirror, rays
parallel to the axis converge after reflection to a
point called the "principal focus," which is half-way
between the center of the sphere and the mirror. Rays
from a luminous object outside the spherical center of

a concave mirror form a small, real, inverted image of the object between the center and the principal focus; when the object is between the center and the principal focus the image is beyond the center, and is large, real, and inverted. (*Encyclopedia Americana,* 1959, p. 222)

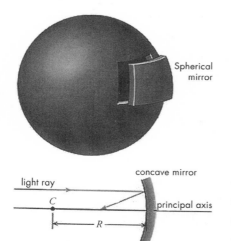

If we are to consider an image other than the one of positive, kataphatic religious experience, I am suggesting that perhaps we explore what it might mean to cross over ontologically and psychologically into the divine abyss. The figure of the spherical mirror gives one possible analogy of what this might look like. Perhaps the axis-in-the-mirror analogy, the point where the rays converge after reflection, gives us some direction as to what might be our "principal focus" in depth psychology. This will correlate with my later discussion on ego-Self axis in Jung's terms and the relationship between the divine and the human in Boehme's terms. I will further explore these terms, axis, and mirror in Boehme's images of the same, which he believes are given to us as tools for locating our principal focus.

Let us take, for now, the image of a concave spherical mirror, thinking in terms of something concave as un-conscious, and how it gives us the notion of below the surface in the way its surface is configured. If the human psyche is to "pass through" as an intersecting plane, which means

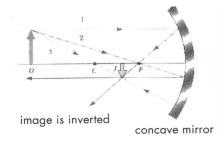

image is inverted

concave mirror

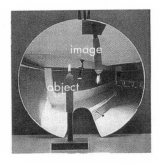

to share in the attributes of the circle of the sphere, then we in some way need to align ourselves with the axis that runs through the center of the spherical surface and meets with the middle point of the mirror. To live in the image, whether kataphatic or apophatic, differentiated or undifferentiated—whatever the expression of religious or primordial experience—the intersection of image with the sphere bearing its potential reflection would occur at the point of convergence called *principal focus*, a convergence that occurs *within* the circumference of the sphere and thus participates in some way with the properties of the sphere. The difference in image would be determined by whether an object is outside the spherical center or between the center and the principal focus.

In either case, outside the spherical center or between the center and the principal focus, when the image is reflected, the image is inverted (fig. 2). The sphere, the originating source of the reflecting capacity, is comprised of a totality, an encompassing circle, but neither image bears the identical properties or attributes of the sphere except in an inverted form.

Both are still viable images but both in some way are in contrast to the original. In terms of being created in "the image of" God, a contrast might imply that the relation between the human being, nature, and spirit is, in some way, the converse of that relation that exists in harmonious balance in God by virtue of its being divided—separated from its origins —(cf. for instance, Martensen, 1949). This is not to imply that we are something negative but to the contrary, that we are given through this contrast, as a form of inner image, as an inside view, the means to reverse what is inverse, to restore an original state.

Nor do I mean to imply by inverted or contrasting that the existence of a positive image is automatically canceled in relation to the other. Both positive image and inverted contrast are constituent parts of what I will be affirming through the symbol abyss as basic reality, the undivided wholeness of the universe. Whether we are speaking of human consciousness, of apophatic or kataphatic theology, I am attesting to the experience of a ground inclusive of a multiplicity of images and contrasts that we experience because they are the realities we are given.

The Abyss

> That which underlies all things [is] the Abyss. This Abyss contains within itself everything and nothing—that is, everything potentially, but nothing manifestly; somewhat as an acorn contains, potentially, a forest of oak trees. (Waite, 1940, pp. 93–94)

Have you ever had an MRI? An MRI, which stands for Magnetic Resonance Imaging, is a medical test in which your body is scanned to show the anatomy of the body from the inside view. You are inserted head-first on a special tray that is slid through a narrow donut-like hole and into the depths of a very large fiberglass machine. The hole you go through is barely two-feet wide and in some cases, smaller. The length of the hole is around twelve-to-fifteen feet. You are slid slowly into the bowels of the machine, which houses a huge cylindrical magnet. A magnetic field is created by the magnet. Magnetic energy conjoined with radio waves echoes or reflects back out of the body images or *contrasts* between healthy and unhealthy tissue.

The idea of being all the way inside this machine conjures up something of what Jonah must have felt like in the belly of the whale. Going inside the belly of the primordial mother inspires panic. Understandably so! Sliding into a narrow hole and being surrounded by metal fuselage with the anticipation of little or no air conjures up breathlessness in the face of the unknown, even images of death. Will there be anything circulating besides a frantic pulse? Is there a dead-end at the far side of the tunnel? Images of what it was like to scurry through a round concrete pipe as a small child pale and are wistfully surrendered.

This procedure begins with an initial descent from a main floor of a building on Columbus Avenue to a floor below the main floor and then again, to a level below the lower level. The first thing you notice at rock-bottom is the sound. Deep below the surface reality of the main floor, reminiscent of the hidden underworld of the Morlocks of H. G. Wells's *Time Machine*, it is as if the caverns of hell have a pulse, a powerful, permeating rumble. Behind a door slightly ajar to the left, the back of a man is visible. He sits in the dark, roboticlike, facing a computer screen of stark black and white images of slices of human anatomy. The level of light on the entire floor is dim, adding to an aura of surreality. There is an intense quiet, a near-silence with the exception of the low-lying beat of an underground generator. An East Indian female technician emerges from the door ahead to the right where the great white whalelike machine lurks.

"Are you ready?" she beckons.

Other MRIs and CAT scans are much smaller in comparison to this Leviathan. This machine is the primal mother: the maternal abyss. She dominates. With the exception of a few feet, the huge machine extends the length of the room and is as high as the ceiling.

Entering this realm of the underworld is to enter the domain of the chthonic primordial maternal. Chthonic refers to dark, concrete, and earthy. On the one hand, the abyss can represent the dark, threatening aspect of the unconscious and the danger of our being swallowed up by it. The abyss can become like a chthonic prison because we are not yet ready to do something that we should (Jung, 1953, par. 277). On the other hand, this chthonic aspect can make itself felt as the fourth function, the inferior aspect of our personality Jung tells us we need to integrate to become whole. This fourth inferior function presents itself as something radically other than the ego's domesticated function, becoming concrete when it needs to be translated, or threatens to translate itself, into reality. Thus, the chasm of the abyss is simultaneously the entrance to the place, the "temple Chthonia," where death has been conquered (Jung, 1956, par. 572) as well as the source of the fear that causes our experience of regression (Ibid., 1968, par. 240).

What does it mean to pray into what is possibly an empty space, empty in the sense of a concrete person, a concrete personal presence? Is the prayer there even if the request has not been received by the person? Does prayer require the flesh of time and space? What is the ultimate manifestation of reception that finally envelopes? What sustains us in being?

I am rolled out of the mouth of the beast. I reflect through my relief that the hole at the other end of the machine that I thought might ease my apprehensions is not the one that has made a difference. The outside hole has helped the air to circulate deep down into the bowels of the machine, but the machine itself is finally a sort of dead-end, closed, or enclosed system. All of us have deep, primordial fears. Whatever these are, I am not sure that there is anything that will completely eradicate these short of knocking us out or rendering us unconscious, or perhaps dying. There seems, however, to be a way to meet the primordial.

The point I wish to make is that for each of us there is a primordial abyss—an unknown place into which we dread to go or to which we may be curiously drawn, or both—and for each of us the abyss will be distinctly and numinously different. The symbol of the abyss or void calls up so many images. Abyss and abysmal often have negative connotations, the notion of Christian Hell, devil, death, oblivion for instance. The notion of abyss can inspire fear and terror, and equally ecstasy, allure, safety and haven. Some people may think of heaven as an abyss into which the personality merges or dissolves in the afterlife. Some individuals seek intentionally to fall into the euphoric hole of a heroin high or another form of substance-induced bliss, which is a kind of abyss as haven. For still others, the abyss of a chaotic and randomly ordered inner world may be the only reality out of which a person can create or locate a sense of creative freedom, however disordered and disconnected externally this state may appear to the rest of us.

If and when in our lives we face an abyss, and I will continue to define it, the fact of unitary reality as something real and personal to us can lead us toward change. We go inside the belly and return with a completely and radically different image of abyss and of ourselves. We come out with a less opaque, more clarified picture of who we are and what we are in the image of. Where our fears had inspired the negative such as in falling or breathlessness, or a negation such as death or not existing, the ultimate end, in reality, is a new beginning and a revisioning of our experience. Our preconceptions are surpassed and our horizons expanded. We come out of the hole knowing that there is something beyond the hole that came from inside but that is not exactly of our making. What we thought would be empty and annihilating is actually full.

I have used the image of the MRI to bring front and center the notion of abyss, to illustrate *inbreaking* on a primordial level in the context of the great reflecting magnet, and to challenge our notion of vision. On the one hand, the abyss calls to mind a reality that cannot even be made a subject when by its nature it pertains to a hidden order, a mystery that is situated beyond our experience. As Raimundo Panikkar says:

> A God who would not be "mysterious" would *eo ipso* cease to be God. Such a God would be a philosophical statement, a target of thought, at most a First Cause—but not God in the meaning ordinarily given to this word. (Panikkar, 1989, p. 165)

On the other hand, just as the magnetic field of an MRI scan gives us an inside view of the body, I believe that at the level of true depth, we can get a glimpse of this hidden order or mystery. We glimpse mystery through a "manifestation of reception."

I have drawn this phrase from a letter that Jung writes to Gerhard P. Zacharias, a Greek Orthodox priest, in which Jung compares the early church father Origen's experience of scripture as Logos to the experience of the unconscious in analytic psychology (Jung, 1975, pp. 120–21). With Jung, a manifestation of reception would pertain to our internal reception of all that is unconscious and our addressing all the layers of otherness of which I have been speaking.

As I mean it, I, too, am referring to an internal reception with an emphasis on active reciprocity between an individual and spirit, as would Jung be from the point of view of analytical psychology in his letter to Father Zacharias. To clarify this notion further, as I think Boehme might intend it, I will draw from Antoine Faivre, a scholar of Boehme.

Faivre speaks of a process of incarnation in which the human soul is "like a female womb ready to receive a spiritual seed with a view to a double pregnancy: not only that of the receiver (the human being), but also that of the giver of seed, who finds himself, by the same token, as though reengendered" (Faivre, p. 160). Manifestation of reception is a two-way street with the constant creation of something fresh. We receive and in our receiving we are received. I will discuss this in chapter six in the context of Boehme's notion of the mirror.

Heinz's "Origin of The Word" must have included This

As in the examples of the two men I will present, my focus is upon the cultivation and development of personal inwardness in the context of personal experience and transformation. I am promoting an extension of consciousness that is not just limited to the rational ground of psychoanalytic, philosophical, or theological work.

I am encouraging an openness to the dimension of depth in which change is concrete and subjective, and begins from within at the dimension of the abyss in which we arrive again at the outside with an inside view. We meet the primordial unitary reality at the abyss of our experience, a place where we also meet our fear, terror, and pain. The fear is not erased but it comes to coexist with something else. If experience of the abyss is real, then this unitary reality is real. The whole thing comes down to our experience. What I am speaking about in terms of descent into the abyss is the reception of all that we are being conjoined at some level with all that is and also with all that is not. These simultaneous realities meet because something is already there on the inside to meet us. It is as if deep calls deep. If this sounds like a paradox, then let me try to explain.

Perhaps one visual analogy of the unitive composite of empty presence—full nothingness is the product of the MRI test itself. A digital computer reconstructs the images or contrasts reflected back so that the inner workings of our body can be seen. From the imprints and contrasts echoed into form, we have a picture of the whole body at least *in image*. We emerge enabled to reconstruct the fact of an inner reality from the reflections of a magnetic field. The invisible becomes visible in some way.

In the actual descent, what is it that unites us in this unitary reality? What finally takes us beyond our images and meets us? Is it our imagination? The revealing of the numinous through the imagination? The numinous, in fact, can inspire images of the abyss as hell or as a range of other experiences. What one person experiences as primordial fear, another might experience entirely differently. There are events similar to MRI scans that are accompanied by similar mechanics that inspire the exact opposite response. Take for instance lying under a glass-enclosed tanning dome, which feels to many as luxuriously nurturing. Or take the example of being submerged below three feet of water in the new giant bathtub-sized hydro-spas, which one patient has claimed to be a delightfully regressive experience of underwater helplessness that helps him to access early trauma.

In fact, the MRI experience perhaps could be experienced similarly by some. Some people just go to sleep during the process. So the role of imagination is complex. The imagination can inspire safety or evoke terror. The imagination is what makes us bold and also the source of our primordial fear. In any case, what becomes evident in an encounter with primordial experience is that we at some point will most likely encounter our opposite, and the imagination will at least be part of this experience.

The special task of depth psychology is to go into the guts of the soul because it is the flesh of the soul that receives what becomes manifest as we go into nondirected, primary-process thinking, archaic thinking, the language of myths, and the unconscious. Without this contact, life withers. Depth psychology brings us in touch again with this archaic level, our roots. It informs our everyday life and the body. In other words, even boldness will need to know fear at some point if boldness is to breathe and to be alive. Even the most frightened child deserves to know solace in a moment of isolated surrender.

Imagination in the context of the primordial plays a significant role in connecting us to what is alive, what is healing. I am exploring at what level it does so. Are there various layers of the imagination, some more healing and sustaining than others, prayer for instance, and the fact of real, concrete persons in our imagination and prayer? Or is the uniting factor something else, and if it is something else, how is this something else transformative and efficacious? Does our experience of unitary reality relate to our full experience of this something else?

Let me define *unitary reality* further. By unitary reality, I am suggesting that at some point in making the unconscious conscious, we come to the realization that the psyche is not possibly all that we are. We use our imagination to glimpse unitary oneness but our imagination, including the contents of the unconscious, is not the same as the unitary reality itself. Thus, the home we eventually discover in the distance of dazzling darkness is not solely the one of our developmental history, our parental introjects, our cultural projections, our political persuasions, our sexual preferences, nor anything else that relates solely to the being of psyche or the being of the created world.

Being, as I am speaking of it here, is the *materia* necessary for our humanness. Being is necessary for us to know that we are, but we must go beyond what we know and what we think we are to receive in the fullest, most manifest form who and what we really are. This is the paradox. Thus, by unitary reality I mean we are relating not only to being but also to a preexisting reality beyond being. Being, if it is not held in tension with its antinomy (its preexistent ground, or un-ground), if it does not include its opposite—what we do not or cannot know in terms of the unknown and mystery—is only part of the individuation journey, the process of becoming whole.

We can glimpse mystery through the image of the abyss as a symbol of unitary reality. I would like to explore how the fact of experience of the abyss may evoke something fresh for all of us in terms of giving us a deepened, widened viewpoint on what happens when our otherness is met by radically other otherness, especially in the context of suffering. The experience of the abyss, like the MRI with its "images and contrasts," may call upon us to re-image, or re-envision, how we relate to our suffering and how our suffering relates to us. This is the relevance to clinical work. Our suffering and how we relate to it also pertain to how we are related to the divine. The notion and experience of abyss may also expand our notion of what it means to be made "in the image" of God and to explore even further how the divine is related to us.

Inevitably, when a person responds to what is experientially real, especially when the experience is powerfully and numinously real for him or her, a statement pops out that bears a certain theological or philosophical import. Certainly, this is the case with each of the persons I will present. Primordial experience is such that I think it can probably do nothing other than cause us to blurt out something passionate in the form of a statement, as have Jung and Boehme, and as *I will*.

Will my statement be theological? In the course of presenting the contents and facts of psychological experience, it could be implied that at some level I am making a statement about something universal that rubs over and against known theological tenets such as the doctrine of revelation, the doctrine of creation, the doctrine of incarnation, for instance. This rub could be implied by virtue of what the facts of the experience of those I am presenting say and also by what the facts of their experience do not say.

Jacob Boehme, for instance, after the fact of his experience of the *Ungrund* speaks of what some have identified as a theology of revelation. Making any statement, however symbolic in its nature, in variance with a sacred doctrine of Christianity, so aggravated the Protestants of his time that he was thrown in prison and his writings were censored. Jung was banished from the psychoanalytic culture, not so much through literal censorship but more through declamations on the part of various theologians and psychologists. His break with Freud over the libido theory certainly made a statement, albeit not a theological one. What Jung refused to say about the divine in his attempt to remain empirical and objective equally got him into a fine stew with theologian Martin Buber and others. In a letter to a graduate student who was analyzing the differences between Buber and himself, Jung claimed,

> I make no transcendental statements. I am essentially empirical, as I have stated more than once. I am dealing with psychic phenomena and not with metaphysical assertions. Within the frame of psychic events I find the fact of the belief in God. It *says:* "God is." This is the fact I am concerned with. I am not concerned

with the truth or untruth of God's existence. (Jung, 1975, p. 570)

Whether or not one makes an actual theological statement, the ramifications will often be the same as if one had. Omission is the fertile ground of projection. My focus is to accept the fact of projection and to go a little further toward understanding something more of the deep strata of psychological experience and its source, which is the very territory of religious experience and of statements of faith. This borderland, not solely the turf of depth psychology nor solely the turf of religion, this shared border of experience will be the point of juncture and conversation. Does what we relate to as *abyss* in the primordial layers of the psyche tell us something about divine presence and/or divine otherness? and, if so, how?

Although I am suggesting that we can point to mystery through what is humanly articulated—that the symbol points—I am still affirming the fact of mystery beyond. Recalling the purpose of the MRI scan to obtain an inside view of the body in contrast form, we can only go into the machine and experience what we experience. We cannot claim that we have the final truth about the "inside view," nor can we claim final truth about the divine.

> I am ready at any time to confess to the inner experience but not to my metaphysical interpretation, otherwise I am implicitly laying claim to universal recognition. On the contrary, I must confess that I cannot interpret the inner experience in its metaphysical reality, since its essential core is of a transcendent nature and beyond my human grasp. (Edinger, 1996, p. 124]

For Jung, transcendence is a relative term pertaining to whatever is unconscious to us. We cannot establish whether this transcendent something is permanently inaccessible to us or only at present. Referring to the past, he reminds us that many things were transcendent that now are the subject matter of science (Ibid., p. 126).

If we interpret the content of experience by a particular faith, we tend to identify with our subjective interpretation of the manifestation, Jung tells us. This is to lay absolute claim, and Jung believes instead that we should interpret by comparing all traditional assumptions of faith without insisting upon one over the other—his emphasis being upon a process that is going on in the unconscious that expresses itself in various images and symbols. We cannot know the exact nature of the content of a vision, "whether it is psychic, whether it comes from an angel or from God himself" (Ibid., p. 126). For Jung, we need to leave these questions open.

In other words, none of us can ever give an interpretation of religious experience or deep experience when confronted with great mystery or "it would no longer be great mystery." On the other hand, in Jung's own confrontation with mystery, he was not slow to pronounce with the cry of ultimacy that comes with the meeting of spirit and matter that there is such a thing as "absolute knowledge."

Absolute knowledge pertains to the existence of an a priori knowledge, a preexisting order, an order before the ego comes to consciousness, before being (Jung, 1960, par. 947). Neumann explains absolute knowledge through a Jewish midrash: "[T]he child, in the mother's womb possesses this absolute knowledge: it can see from one end of the world to the other. It is not until birth that, by the intervention of an angel, it losses its original gift of vision" (Neumann, 1989, p. 81).

Neumann goes on to connect absolute knowledge with Jung's Self-field, defining absolute knowledge as the formally directing fact that activates and directs the archetypal field "as a deeper regulating and ordering field" (Ibid., pp. 47–49).

James Olney concurs that the Self reflects absolute knowledge as it contains the merging of the opposites of consciousness and unconsciousness in a marriage, a *hieros gamos*, a unified One. In this Unity of Being, "because the microcosm is identical with the macrocosm, it attracts the latter and this brings about a kind of apocatastasis, a restoration of…the original wholeness" (Olney, 1980, p. 323). Absolute knowledge is Self-knowledge, knowledge of the Self, which is a remembering of the *homo totus*, the Son of God, as an archetypal idea "by definition universal in occurrence and capable of autochthonous revival anywhere at anytime (Ibid., p. 323). What we *re-member* in absolute knowledge is our origins. We re-member through *anamnesis*, "a memory of wholeness and an apocastasis that restores wholeness" (Ibid., p. 323).

I am asking us to hold this continuum of experience-mystery while we begin to explore some of the contents of the psyche. What is transcendent (at least in Jung's terms) may be reducible to our psychological categories although mystery itself as the source of what we experience as transcendent may not be reducible. What are we then to make of claims such as "absolute knowledge"? I am claiming that mystery may be related to our experience. We exist in relation to mystery but we do not create it.

At the same time, we can still create and be creative. We have been graced with the human faculties of the collective unconscious, the imagination, our experience, and the fact of images and contrasts within us. The unconscious acts compensatorily to depict what we are not conscious of. We can speculate that if the archetypal expression of a particular symbol keeps coming up in the human psyche throughout the history of human consciousness, that this expression may offer us the content or contrast of what we normally do relate to. In fact, Jung says:

> [T]hat the unconscious does not simply act *contrary* to the conscious mind but *modifies* it more in the manner of an opponent or partner. The son type does not call up a daughter as a complementary image from the depths of the "chthonic" unconscious—it calls up another son. (1968, par. 26)

Think of this in terms of dynamic inbreaking of the collective unconscious and glimpses of eternity, and place the notion of spirit coming toward us, summoning us, in conjunction with culture, the unfolding of human history.

I believe that the abyss as a repeated expression of unitary reality in the psyche is emblematic of what is unconscious and needs to be made conscious again and again in our intrapsychic and collective lives as a symbol of individuation. And what rises from the abyss, this "star" incarnates both individually and collectively in human history. The star, as it was a symbol to the wise men of ancient times, is the symbol of history's eschatological fulfillment. As Boehme and Jung attest, the star is born in us individually and personally when we recognize it inwardly and allow it to give birth to the fullness of our inner contents. The inner world is also the flesh of the outer world, in fact a flesh transformed. The birth of the star is the birth of an *other*, the birth of a contrast that paradoxically is sameness, likeness "in the image" of the divine, the paradox Jung speaks of in "the birth of another son."

Thus, I am supporting through the presentation of the abyss symbol an interpretation of what it might mean to live not only in the image of our images, but also in the image of what is beyond our images. The abyss symbol may help us to understand how our dealing with contrast and otherness from the inside view informs how we deal with otherness outside, culturally and historically, in the course of the individuation process.

> In relation to what is "not yet," we come to know who and what we are in the way of the Lonely One's gaze into the void, the abyss, a bottomless depth from which the star is born.

3

Radical Otherness

"The Absolute is a definitive mystery.
God is transcendental; an abyss separates man
from Him.
But the transcendental nature of God is our imma-
nent experience." (BERDYAEV, 1946, PP. 52, 46)

"We must say yes to the spirit even if we do not know
it. The spirit in spirit knows us. If we are open to
spirit, it pours down on us. Do we contemplate the
world we live in? Do we thrust ourselves with pas-
sion into the crucial textures of the world?" (BARRY
ULANOV, personal communication, June 10, 1999)

THUS FAR, I have considered otherness in terms of projective and introjective otherness: the *me* and *not me*
of the psyche. I have spoken of some of the subject and
object distinctions we make that, in their more limited
form, reflect in culture as objectification and depersonalization. On a philosophical level, I have described Ricœur's
Wholly Other in contrast to the religious object in the context of his philosophy of immanence and his philosophy of
transcendence.

I have also indicated that the Wholly Other may, in
truth, be beyond all of our categories of understanding.

The Wholly Other may be a *radically other* other, beyond even what we conceptualize as *being* in the metaphysical sense. If we are to raise to consciousness a full understanding of otherness, then we would do well to consider images or symbols that are typically overlooked in the contemporary conversation on "otherness." These images reveal an authentic depth that points beyond it to a pre-existent, totally transcendent ultimacy.

Let me now turn, in this and the following chapter, to images of radically other otherness in the experience and writings of Boehme and Jung. I begin by offering the numinous experiences of these two extraordinary visionaries, separated by three centuries but conjoined by the intensity and similarity of the inner experiences that they shared, the work that they produced in response to these experiences, and the people that they influenced.

In this chapter, I present Jacob Boehme: his external influences, inner conflicts, and his images of the Abyss, or the *Ungrund*. In the next chapter, I explore the experiences of the Pleroma of Carl Jung. As with Boehme, I will also examine the external influences and inner conflicts that preceded and surrounded Jung's experiences. I am emphasizing the kind of experience that informs us in an *inner way*, the experience of dreams and the imagination that comes forth as the deeply unconscious is made conscious.

The images that I present in my discussion of the experiences of Boehme and Jung—the abyss/*Ungrund*, and the Pleroma—share the fact that they express a unitary reality. I am asserting that unitary reality underlies all psychological experience of which these images are an expression. The examples of unitary reality that I offer are sometimes a single event but most often the culmination of numerous events following a long period of struggle and suffering.

Unitary reality is more likely a culmination of a long-term process of encounter with the deepest layer of the collective unconscious, the psychoid, archetypal layer in which we meet all forms of otherness, and potentially, radically other otherness through which we find our ground, and the reality that bridges us to this ground: Christ for Boehme, the Self for Jung.

The Self-revealing of this reality gets our attention one way or another. If the ego becomes oriented toward this reality and what links us to it, the linking-Christ, the bridging-Self (which are two different realities but express the same bridging principle), these ever-present but independent guides continue to reveal the generative mystery of the life-giving void or abyss. In relation to them, we begin to live creatively. We are able to shape and fashion the raw material given us in relation to a deeper layer of being that sustains us.

Unitary Reality

Boehme and Jung—each in their own experience of depth, and each in their own vision of it—tell us something of what exists there. By depth, I am referring to diving beyond what we know to radical otherness and letting what is found there inform us. The depth I am describing is reminiscent of apophatic mystical experience in which the experience is one of the ego having died or fallen away.

In *Alchemical Studies*, Jung talks of this experience. He relates that he, himself, knows of "a few individuals" who have experienced this state. Could he have been drawing from his own experience of the collective unconscious in the following passage? We might be tempted to think so:

> So far as I have been able to understand it, it seems to have to do with an acute state of consciousness, as intense as it is abstract, a "detached" consciousness, which, as Hildegard implies, brings into awareness areas of psychic happenings ordinarily covered in darkness. The fact that the general bodily sensations disappear during the experience suggests that their specific energy has been withdrawn and has apparently gone towards heightening the clarity of consciousness. As a rule, the phenomenon is spontaneous, coming and going on its own initiative. Its effect is astonishing in that it almost always brings about a solution of psychic complications and frees the inner personality from emotional and intellectual entanglements, thus creating a *unity of being* that is universally felt as "liberation." (Jung, 1983, par. 43)

Because mystery can be represented only symbolically, I will, in most cases, present this material—the *Ungrund*, the dark void of the abyss, and the Pleroma—in the form that is closest to the original, i.e., in the unanalyzed, direct words of the one who had the experience.

Inspired by what each experienced to be authentic and real, each man's consciousness of radical otherness begins with an apprehension of a unitary reality, one that is subsequently shattered into opposites before reuniting with its original ground (or un-ground). In relation to the instinctual field of numinous, archetypal experience, each brings to consciousness a notion of abyss that shows us that the images we think we know are possibly not all that we are.

What I shall expand upon below will not so much be the notion of the "abyss of hell" in the imagery of the Christian tradition as it will the abyss (described variously as Pleroma and *Ungrund*) as a symbol of a preexistent, unitary reality. Boehme and Jung offer us, through what is authentically real for them, a reality perhaps analogous to Martin Buber's "divine Void" (Neumann, p. 114). The abyss or divine Void is a Self-revealing reality that gives life to the world but is itself a mystery (Ibid., p. 115). It gives life by penetrating and uniting the human being to layers of existence that exist in and through and beyond the human psyche.

Jacob Boehme and the Abyss

Jacob Boehme was certainly not the first, nor clearly the last to have had a vision of the abyss as something other than a "hell mouth." As an example, the vision of a patient of Frances Wickes, related below, is stunning, even beautiful, in its stark clarity and mythological feel:

> I looked upon space and I beheld darkness. In that darkness moved mysterious forces. Not like the gods of man's conceiving were they, but strange primeval beings born before the gods of human form. They were hooded in darkness. Through their fingers they drew the threads of blackness and ever wove them back and forth. I saw the rays that they made like the rays that stream inward from a many-pointed star or the converging of the lines of a many-sided crystal, but these rays were not of light but of darkness, and the darkness seemed to draw all things into it. Thus I knew that they were weaving a great void that had no form nor boundaries. (Wickes, 1950, p. 245)

Boehme had similarly alluring visions, illuminations, and deep experiences of God and nature, from which he produced a series of profound writings that influenced a lineage of theologians, mystics, artists, philosophers and psychologists to the present day. These visions, and the writings that followed, though, caused Boehme to be rejected by his church and exiled from his hometown as a pathetic and misguided heretic.

Although these experiences were of a *radically other* reality, one beyond time and space, it is, nonetheless, important to appreciate something of the time (1575–1624) and place (Görlitz in eastern Germany) in which Boehme lived and wrote, for these experiences do not occur in a vacuum. The final quarter of the seventeenth century was characterized by intense political and religious upheaval. It was a liminal time, a "hinge period when old certainties were destroyed and thinking people felt inclined to face two ways; striving to save something from the past and yet fascinated and exhilarated by the prospects of new forms of living held out to them by the future" (Waterfield, 1989, p. 17). Barely a generation had passed since Luther had set the Reformation ball rolling down its inexorable path, causing the Western Church to begin its eventual splitting into myriad permutations. A mere twelve years before Boehme's birth, the Council of Trent concluded by inaugurating a fierce Counter-Reformation. The tensions between these opposing forces would lead to the burning at the stake or the banishment throughout Europe of thousands of "heretics."

If the historical era into which Boehme was born was particularly significant to his formation, the place of his birth, the village of Old Seidenberg near Görlitz, in eastern

Germany, was also. During Boehme's lifetime, Görlitz served as a haven for many who sought refuge from the religious strife of the times.

Discovering himself to be physically unsuited to the farming work of his ancestors, Boehme was drawn to the trade of a cobbler. Upon completing his apprenticeship he began his "journeyman travels" throughout Upper Lusatia, a "land torn by dissension, party strife, and religious unrest." In fact, the conflict was so severe that "in 1592, the year Boehme's travels began, Rudolf of Saxony ordered a thoroughgoing religious purge" of the area (Stoudt, 1957, p. 47). Six years before Boehme died, these tensions would eventually flare up into the Thirty Years' War, which scorched the central European countryside with the flames of religious conflict.

By 1600, Boehme had been back home in Görlitz for five years and had established himself as a businessman, having recently purchased a "cobbler's bench" from the man whose sister he was to marry the very next month. Later that year, Boehme was to have one of the most significant of his illuminations.

In addition to being the beginning of a new century, the year 1600 was significant for Boehme in many respects. In January, his wife Katherina, gave birth to their first child, a son they named Jacob. A new chief pastor, Martin Moller, was installed at Boehme's church. That first year of his service, Pastor Moller organized a study group called the "Conventicle of God's Real Servants." Boehme became a member of the group and began to learn much from Moller who was "the author of numerous works of a mystical nature that owed much to the Fathers of the Church, notably St. Augustine, and to a very wide range of later mystical writers" (Waterfield, 1989, p. 21).

But the year 1600 was notable in Europe for another reason—the weather:

> This was indeed a fateful year. Even the weather was erratic. On Easter a great snow came down and the cold lingered long into the spring. It was only a week before Whitsunday that the cattle could be taken from their stalls into the open fields and the trees still had no leaves. The cherry trees were not in bloom until Trinity Sunday. (Stoudt, 1957, p. 49)

It was sometime during the Spring of this "fateful year" that Jacob had a "shattering mystical experience that became the vital center of his life and thought" (Stoudt, 1957, p. 56). The experience was as profound as it was brief, lasting a mere fifteen minutes. Nonetheless, it provided Boehme with material for thought and writing for years to come. As he, himself, described the experience,

> the gate was opened unto me, that in one-quarter of an hour I saw and knew more than if I had been many years together at a University; at which I did exceedingly admire, and I knew not how it happened to me; and thereupon I turned my heart to praise God for it. (Waterfield, 1989, pp. 63–64)

As recounted in *Aurora*, his first major writing produced some twelve years after the vision, "My spirit directly saw through all things, and knew God in and by all creatures, even in herbs and grass....In this light my will grew in great desire to describe the being of God" (Boehme, 1915, xix, p. 13).

What was the nature of this experience that revealed to Boehme the "Being of all Beings, the Byss (the ground or original foundation), and Abyss (what is without ground, or bottomless and fathomless)..." (Waterfield, 1989, p. 64)? It is described in the following passage by Hans Martensen, one of Boehme's biographers:

> Sitting one day in his room, his eye fell upon a burnished pewter dish, which reflected the sunshine with such marvelous splendor that he fell into an inward ecstasy, and it seemed to him as if he could now look into the principles and deepest foundations of things. He believed that it was only a fancy, and in order to banish it from his mind he went out into the green fields. But here he noticed that he could gaze into the very heart of things, the very herbs and grass, and that actual nature harmonized with what he had inwardly seen. (Martensen, 1949, p. 5)

In *Wisdom's Children: A Christian Esoteric Tradition*, Arthur Versluis speaks most interestingly of the fact that "Boehme's revelation was preceded by a period of deep melancholy, during which he had been in a profound quandary over the existence of evil and suffering in the world" (Versluis, 1999, p. 4). In Boehme's own words from *Aurora*, written more than a decade after the fact, we see something of the psychic struggles that consumed him at the time of the vision.

> [A]t last I fell into a very deep melancholy and heavy sadness, when I beheld and contemplated the great deep of this world, also the sun and stars, the clouds, rain and snow, and considered in my spirit the whole creation of this world.

Wherein then I found to be in all things, evil and good, love and anger, in the inanimate creatures, viz. in wood, stones, earth and the elements, as also in men and beasts.

Moreover, I considered the little spark of light, man, what he should be esteemed for with God, in comparison with this great work and fabric of heaven and earth.

But finding that in all things there was evil and good, as well in the elements as in the other creatures, and that it went as well in this world with the wicked as with the virtuous, honest, and Godly; also that the barbarous people had the best countries in their possession, and that they had more prosperity in their ways than the virtuous, honest and Godly had.

I was thereupon very melancholy, perplexed and exceedingly troubled, no Scripture could comfort or satisfy me, though I was very well acquainted with it, and versed therein. (Boehme, 1915, pp. 485–87)

It was then in the context of this intense inner struggle, perhaps mirroring the religious storms in the outside world in which Boehme lived, that he was able to penetrate through the clouds to another layer of being. He continues in *Aurora*:

But when in this affliction and trouble I elevated my spirit (for I then understood very little or not at all what it was), I earnestly raised it up into God, as with a great storm or onset, wrapping up my whole heart and mind, as also all my thoughts and whole will and resolution, incessantly to wrestle with the love and mercy of God, and not to give over, until he blessed me, that is, until he enlightened me with his holy spirit, whereby I might understand his will, and

be rid of my sadness. And then the spirit did break
through. (Ibid.)

So overjoyed with the lightening of his melancholy (depression), he found it difficult to "express, either in speaking
or in writing" what he described as the "triumphing of the
spirit." He even went so far as to liken the experience to
"the resurrection from the dead" (Ibid., p. 488).

Was it melancholy brought on by the unresolved conflict (internal or external) and exacerbated by an exceedingly long and gloomy winter that triggered this experience of enlightenment? Was it the influential, mentoring
presence of Pastor Moller with his mystical interests that
catalyzed an inbreaking of the spirit in his oppressed soul?
Was it both? It is hard to know precisely because Jacob
Boehme did not commit to writing the content of his experiences until twelve years after the sunlight on the pewter
jar had opened these inner gates to him. His explanation
for this interval is that he "could not at once apprehend the
deepest births of God in their being, and comprehend them
in my reason." As a result, "there passed almost twelve
years, before the exact understanding thereof was given
me" (Ibid., p. 488).

Of all the themes that Boehme explored in his voluminous writings, the most profound is that of a groundless abyss, beyond the created world, beyond even God
as we know and think of God. This abyss he termed the
Ungrund (un-ground). Boehme was drawn to a new creation myth that expanded and complemented the Genesis
story. In the image of the *Ungrund* he uncovered such a
myth. It is in *Aurora* that he first broaches the theme of
beginnings:

Many authors have written that heaven and earth were created out of nothing. But I wonder that, among so many excellent men, there hath not one been found that could yet describe the true ground; seeing the same God that now is, hath been from eternity. (Ibid., pp. 500–501)

Perceiving both a vacuum and a need, he takes on the self-identified calling of describing "the true ground" in the balance of his opus. In *Signatura Rerum*, Boehme speaks of the "Grand Mystery of All Beings":

We give you to understand this of the divine essence; without nature God is a mystery, understand in the nothing, for without nature is the nothing, which is an eye of eternity, an abyssal eye, that stands or sees in the nothing, for it is the abyss; and this same eye is a will, understand a longing after manifestation, to find the nothing; but now there is nothing before the will, where it might find something, where it might have a place to rest, therefore it enters into itself, and finds itself in nature. (1969, p. 22)

The true ground of God is, then, to Boehme an *unground* or *Ungrund*. It is a theme he pursued in work after work, including his *magnum opus*, the three-volume *Mysterium Magnum*, which was written in the last years of his life. In the following passage, however, Boehme introduces a new theme. Here he equates the *nothing* with the *all*. The *emptiness* is also the *fullness*; both beyond space and time, the *abyss* is also the Pleroma. (This concept has particular relevance to Jung's experience of Pleroma that became the basis for his *Septem Sermones*, which I explore in depth in the following chapter.)

The eternal divine understanding is a free will, not arisen either from any thing or by any thing; it is its own peculiar seat, and dwelleth only and alone in itself, un-apprehended of any thing; for beyond and without it is nothing, and that same NOTHING is only ONE; and yet it is also as a nothing to itself. It is one only will of the abyss, and it is neither near nor far off, neither high nor low; but it is ALL, and yet as a Nothing. For there is in itself no contemplation, sensation or perceivancy whereby it might find a likeness in itself. (1965, p. 217)

In *The Way to Christ*, a series of treatises also written toward the end of his life, Boehme intimately reveals something about his early experience, which was to inspire these writings. He speaks of the importance of stillness in the soul of one seeking direct experience of God.

If it were possible for him to remain quiet for an hour or less in his inner self-will and speaking, the divine will would speak into him. Through this inspeaking, God's will forms His will in man in Himself, and speaks into the formed, natural, essential, external life of reason and smashes the earthly formation of the rational will, and enlightens it so that immediately the supersensual divine life and will sprouts in the rational will and centers itself in it. (1978, p. 209)

Could this interval of an "hour or less" be a specific reference to Boehme's own fifteen-minute inbreaking of the spirit—an inspeaking of God's will—triggered by the sunlight on the pewter dish some two decades previous? If so, further evidence of the nature of that "shattering" experience follows:

> For if life stands quiet in its own willing, when it stands in the *abyss of nature and creature* [emphasis mine], in the eternal speaking out of God, then God speaks in it.
>
> Life then went forth from God's speaking, and came into the body, and is nothing other than the formed will of God. If now one's own self-image and willing are still, divine forming and willing will rise up. For whatever is without will is one thus with the nothing and is beyond all nature, which abyss is God Himself. (Ibid., p. 209)

Here, Boehme seems to connect his illuminative experience directly with the concept of the abyss or the *Ungrund*. This would indicate that the concept was "inspired" from the experience as opposed to being "reasoned" through the rational mind. As we will see, this notion of shaping a concept inspired by "spirit breaking in" is very similar to Jung's development of the theory of the collective unconscious around the inbreaking image of the Pleroma.

The abyss, for Boehme, is a "place" beyond time and space from which emanate all possibilities. It is an "eternal speaking," of God, a "breathing out of Himself" from which all creation arises. This breathing "speaks through the static ground of life" and is a "likeness of the divine breathing" (Ibid, p. 209).

Boehme frequently sought to complement the Genesis creation story with one of the creation of being from pre-being, of something from nothing. This creation myth goes beyond the standard "God created the world *ex nihilo.*" It articulates a process in which God created God's self from the nothingness of the abyss through an eternal will. In his essay on Boehme in A. E. Waite's *Three Famous Mystics,*

W. P. Swainson describes a version of this "creation myth" by which God differentiates himself out of the nothingness of the abyss.

> This Will, or Byss, fashions what is called a Mirror, which reflects all things, everything existing already in a latent or hidden state in the Abyss. It thereby makes them visible or manifest. The Supreme thus, as it were, perceives all things in Himself. The dual principle is latent in Him. He is both Byss and Abyss. He could not otherwise know Himself. The manifest is equally eternal with the unmanifest, there never having been a period without manifestation. Boehme terms this Mirror the Eternal Wisdom, the Eternal Idea, or the Virgin Sophia. It is the Infinite Mother, the Will being the Infinite Father.
>
> From this Duality proceeds a Trinity. The Father-Mother begets the Son, in Whom His-Her energies are concentrated or gathered up.... Manifestation is brought about by what Boehme calls Eternal Nature. When the Will, or the Father, beholds Himself and his wonders reflected in the Eternal Idea or Virgin Sophia, the Mother, He desires that they shall not merely remain passive or hidden, but become active and manifest. The Mother also yearns for the manifestation of the marvels latent in Her. Through the union of the Will and the Wisdom, the Father and the Mother, the generation of all things takes place, the unmanifest becomes manifest, the latent becomes active. (Waite, 1940, pp. 93–95)

Just to give a visual analogy, let us recall the diagram and image of the mirror in chapter two. We might conceive of Boehme's Will or Byss as a wondrous sphere that perceives "all things in Himself." This sphere is bounded by a "surface" (here meaning, all things manifest and visible), which is everywhere equally distant from a central point. Visually, we might think of the Mirror of Eternal Wisdom, Sophia, as a spherical mirror that is a manifest portion of the surface of the sphere co-eternal with the "sphere." The Trinity proceeds from the union of the two and the unmanifest becomes manifest as a "reflection" of the union of the Will and the Idea.

To offer a spin on the manifestation of this union, note that a spherical mirror does not "reflect" anything unless it has an object or "plane" that intersects its field. In the above creation myth, Boehme claims a similar notion. "He could not otherwise know Himself," refers to a kind of consciousness that becomes manifest in the Eternal Mirror. Without something other to be conscious of it, everything in the abyss existing in a latent state would remain hidden.

For God to realize himself concretely he must have an object. The differentiation that exists at the birth of the Trinity "is still an act of the spirit...the Trinity does not yet exist concretely. Until the creation of the world, which is the other of God, the One now manifested in the Trinity is only an idea of God's potential concrete form. It is through the relation with the other, the world, that God accomplishes his own self-revelation" (McLachlan, 1992, p. 128).

Jung says something similar, borrowing from the language of religion while expressing the notion of other in psychological form. Jung says that Christ is an event that has always existed in eternity as an eternal process that appears again and again in time in an irregular pattern (1958, par. 629), time being relative to the nontemporality of the *Ungrund* (or for Jung, the Pleroma). Although Christ is already born in the pleroma, his birth in time can be accomplished only when it is perceived, recognized, and declared by human-kind (1958, par. 748). As I have said earlier in the context of the ego-Self sphere (or axis), Jung places emphasis upon the notion of consciousness and the importance of the ego as this necessary other. The ego's consciousness of Self is crucial for the Self to become present in the world.

Moved to bring to conscious expression the "eternal speaking," Boehme sought to describe in detail what his "inspired" writings were like in one of his numerous letters to a friend, saying,

> I might sometimes write more elegantly, but the fire burning within me is driving me on. My hand and my pen must then seek to follow the thoughts as well as they can. The inspiration comes like a shower of rain. That which I catch I have. If it were possible to grasp and describe all that I perceive, then would my writings be more explicit. (Alleman, 1932, pp. 28–29)

These visions were so profound that George Mervin Alleman, in his 1932 doctoral dissertation, "A Critique of Some Philosophical Aspects of the Mysticism of Jacob Boehme," writes that even had Boehme been "familiar with modern psychological terminology," it would not have helped him very much to "explain his very real inspiration and experience" (Ibid., pp. 28–29).

Had Dr. Alleman, himself, been familiar with the "psychological terminology" of his twentieth-century contemporary, Carl Jung, he might not have made such a sweeping statement. Despite the many references in Jung's *Collected Works* to Boehme, Alleman makes not a single reference to Jung in his dissertation, even in a chapter somewhat dubiously entitled "Some Psychological Aspects of the

Mysticism of Jacob Boehme." Jung's appropriation of the language of alchemy in his explanation of the psychological process of individuation would have been very familiar territory to Boehme. One is tempted to think that, had Boehme read the works of Jung or known him, he would have recognized in his writings a similar map to his own inner journey.

Boehme's experiences not only inspired a significant opus of work from his own pen, but they (and his writings) also influenced generations of other mystics, theologians, philosophers, psychologists, and even artists and musicians. A comprehensive Boehme bibliography from the Boehme Resource page on the Internet lists over 700 published works written about or related to Boehme since his death in 1624. In the last hundred years alone, some 504 books, dissertations, monographs, articles, reviews, and chapters have been written, including a dissertation, entitled *Zur Geschichte Des Individuationsproblem (Nicolaus von Cues und Jakob Böhme)*, written by Martin Buber in 1904 for his doctorate at the University of Vienna.

Twentieth-century Russian philosopher Nicolas Berdyaev is one of those who was greatly influenced by the experiences and writings of Boehme. I find Berdyaev both a useful explicator of Boehme and one who, inspired by Boehme, makes something of his concept of the *Ungrund*. Berdyaev develops his understanding of spirit and freedom directly from Boehme's image of the primal, preexistential *Ungrund*.

The *Ungrund* is a fathomless abyss of pre-being because it precedes the being of created essence and form. In other words, something exists that precedes essence. The *Ungrund* is the no-thing, a pure potentiality, a freedom that is as yet undetermined. The *Ungrund* is the free nothing out of which God creates, a freedom of endless possibilities. It is the abyss out of which all things come into being (Berdyaev, 1935, p. 73). In *The Meaning of History*, he puts it this way:

> Somewhere in immeasurable greater depths, there exists a state that may be called *Ungrund*, or "ground-lessness," to which neither human words nor the categories of good and evil, nor those of being or non-being are applicable. *Ungrund* is deeper than anything else and is the primal source of what, according to Boehme and Schelling, constitutes the *Dark Nature of God*. In the nature of God, deeper than Him, lies a theogonic process or that of divine genesis. This process is secondary when compared with the primal "groundlessness" and inexpressible abyss which is irrational and incommensurable with any of our categories. There is a primal source and fount of being from which an eternal torrent pours and in which the divine light shines everlastingly, while the act of divine genesis is taking place. (Berdyaev, 1936, pp. 54–55)

In other words, before the process of "divine genesis," echoing Boehme, Berdyaev says that there is a primary, preexistent *Ungrund*. The theogonic, self-birthing of God is a secondary event that happens in a torrential flooding of being from pre-being. Creation *ex nihilo*, then pertains both to God and the cosmos.

Like Boehme, Berdyaev sees the *Ungrund* as another sort of actuality altogether than the being of the known God; an actuality that gives meaning to existence rather than being merely a layer or part of existence.

Contemporary philosophers Paul Ricœur and Emmanual Levinas articulate a similar notion to Berdyaev and Boehme's. The actuality of spirit is primary and beyond being, and is inexpressible by our usual categories. For Ricœur, we witness this actuality by "letting go of absolute claims." In so doing, we allow for something else to come to pass, namely, an originary affirmation of the absolute by which he means that the absolute in its generosity appears as revelation without a "pretension of consciousness," consciousness that is self-conscious or in which symbols are too quickly turned into ideal forms (Ricœur, 1980, pp. 109–111).

For Levinas, revelation occurs the moment when the pretension of consciousness is dismantled and the radical alterity of the other comes into view as radically other (Levinas, 1969, p. 195). We witness the Infinite as revelation, but witness is an exception to the rule of being. The Infinite is of an order that cannot be represented adequately. A moment occurs that discloses an abyss, a moment of temporary dismembering in terms of self-forgetting in which something other than being comes to pass. "The witness belongs to the glory of the Infinite. It is by the voice of witness that the glory of the Infinite is glorified" (Levinas, 1981, p. 146).

For Berdyaev, a twentieth-century witness, the important point is that spirit is truly free and is the means to personal freedom of human beings. We observe spirit in the creation of ever-new being (Berdyaev, 1946, p. 57).

At the deepest level, the *Ungrund* cannot be characterized at all except as "*ewiges Kontrarium.*" In Boehme's visions, these eternal contrarieties exist and emerge together: from *Abyss* to *Byss.* As Swainson relates,

Boehme calls that which underlies all things the Abyss. This Abyss contains within Itself everything and nothing—that is, everything potentially, but nothing manifestly; somewhat as an acorn contains, potentially, a forest of oak trees. Hidden, as it were, within this Abyss is an eternal, bottomless, uncreated Will, or Byss. This Will, or Byss, ever desires to become manifest—"It willeth to be somewhat." This is only possible in a state of duality or differentiation, for without contrast there could only be eternal stillness, nothing could ever be perceived. (Waite, 1940, pp. 93–94)

Boehme finds the *Ungrund* at the very depth of God—his vision is a kind of *depth theology*. The *Ungrund* is anterior to God and anterior to Being. Recalling Boehme's vision of the eye in the pewter plate, Boehme says that the *Ungrund* lies in the eye, the core of God and creation (Boehme, 1969, 3:1, 16:16). *The Ungrund* is eternally a mystery to God because it is *what God was before God became conscious of God's Self.* The *Ungrund* is predistinction, preexistent. In this sense, it is eternal silence because, even though it contains all the antinomies, all the contradictions are still in harmony, because they are only potential—like the acorn of Swainson's analogy—but not yet differentiated. Thus, the *Ungrund* is not the personal creator God but the absolute-in-itself, a moment at the commencement of the divine life and process of self-creation and revelation of Being and the divine (Boehme, 1965, 1:1).

In the following chapter, I explore the *Nekyia* of Carl Jung, the six-year journey into the dark underworld of the unconscious that not only inspired many of his major theories (the collective unconscious, anima-animus, synchronicity, the shadow, and so forth), but was also directly responsible for producing one of Jung's most interesting, and most misunderstood works, *Septem Sermones ad Mortuos.* There are parallels here to the experiences of Jacob Boehme. Jung, in fact, does draft a psychological map for greater understanding not only of his own inner journey, but also that of Boehme and anyone else so blessed or cursed (for it is a place of "ewiges Kontrarium") to be drawn there.

4

Jung and the Pleroma

I NOW TURN TO images of the abyss, which Jung called
Pleroma in his experience and writings. Pleroma for Jung
is similar to and different from the Boehmean abyss. In his
Collected Works, Jung offers various images of the abyss,
drawn from the wealth of Gnostic and alchemical literature (1959a, par. 578; 1958, par. 255; 1989, par. 8), from
hero myths (1966, par. 261), as well as those images seen
through the traditional lens of Christian theology.

In traditional Christian imagery, the abyss is the gap-
ing hole of Hell, first clearly seen in the New Testament
where Satan "appears as the adversary of Christ, and with
him we gaze for the first time into the luminous realm of
divinity on the one hand and into the abyss of Hell on the
other." Jung also refers to the early Christian linking of
the abyss (or Hell) with the sea, quoting St. Hilary who
says that "the depths of the sea" is equivalent to "the seat
of hell." The sea is the "gloomy abyss," the remains of the
original pit, and hence "the chaos that covered the earth"
(1958, par. 254).

Jung relates that, for St. Augustine, this abyss is the
realm of power allotted to the devil and demons after the
fall. It is on the one hand a "deep that cannot be reached or
comprehended" and on the other the "depths of sin." For

Gregory the Great the sea is the "depths of eternal death" (1989, par. 255). It is, quite clearly, a place to be avoided at all costs.

What I wish to emphasize, however, is not so much the objective image of abyss presented and explored throughout the *Collected Works* and Jung's other writings, but more so his personal encounter with the abyss during the years 1913 to 1916. These were years of breakdown and breakthrough encompassing personal episodes often more reflective of agony than ecstasy, long months reduced to days, sometimes one at a time, and buoyed of the flesh of creative play, the building of a miniature stone village complete with a church, single acts of singular focus.

A direct encounter with the chthonic noumenal of what Jung later came to call the collective unconscious inspires gratitude even when we are caught in the momentum, the spiraling vortex of overwhelming gravity. There are times when we are grateful just to know who exactly it is that we are on any given day. What is my name? What are my degrees? Whom do I live with? And how do I believe myself to locate meaning today? These are some of the kinds of questions Jung asked of himself in and around December 1913.

There are persons throughout history whose lengthy recounts speak to how they have felt victimized or persecuted by the upsurge of the contents of the unconscious. In an "anything but this" telltale escape from their inner contents, these persons successfully hail the nearest ship and voyage off on a great sail, topping the whitecaps of the great sea, never to "dive" beneath its ruthless tides. Perhaps they are smarter and saner for it.

Then there are individuals who feel summoned on a "journey to the beyond," to borrow a phrase from Marie Louise von Franz (1975, p. 110), and who lean into the sail of what feels to them to be the center of the lifestream. They go into the wind, sometimes against it, attempting to navigate these sometimes-gravely irrational waters with a sort of suffering aliveness, not in a masochistic way, but with a certain passion and gusto. Their *caleo*, or call, is, as a friend and mentor once told me, "to dig into their inner contents." They do so by getting in and licking out the substantial marrow from the inside (Madden, 2001, p. 191).

At the same time, being summoned to a journey beyond may be less one of vocation and more one based upon a collective tide. Interestingly, those whom I am offering as eyewitnesses to inner events, Boehme and Jung, came to maturity in times of revolution and upheaval in Europe: post-Reformation and the Thirty Years' War; post-Industrial Revolution and two world wars. There was a disturbance of the collective during the lives of both, of monumental proportions.

JUNG'S NEKYIA

Many creative people are summoned as vessels through which new insights are made manifest of a consciousness higher or more satisfactory than the one that previously existed. They are our prophets of culture, prophets who I would identify specifically as explorers of this great sea of the unconscious. Von Franz attributes Jung's dreams of catastrophe just prior to the outbreak of World War I to his prophetic role. He would have renounced this role and in fact, did so, although he would have admitted to being a vehicle, a crucible for the transmission of unconscious contents especially during the time of these six years.

Von Franz (1975), drawing from anthropologist and scholar Mircea Eliade, likens Jung to the shaman whose "main function is the healing of personal illnesses and disturbances in the life of the collective" (Eliade, 1964, p. 8 passim), explaining that a shaman often suffers from the plight of his people. Like the shaman or medicine man, certain individuals are forced into a particular inner way as a result of the collective culture around them. The shaman's journey

> is "generally heralded by a period of psychic disorientation." As he feels summoned, "he sets himself apart, turns contemplative; often he receives his call through a dream experience." (Ibid., p. 21)

This psychic disorientation is exactly what we see in Jung right after his break with Freud. During that time, Jung was plagued and perplexed. In his own words, he describes the psychic turmoil:

> After the parting of the ways with Freud, a period of inner uncertainty began for me. It would be no exaggeration to call it a state of disorientation. I felt totally suspended in mid-air, for I had not yet found my own footing. (1963, p. 170)

Von Franz goes on to describe the not-uncommon phenomenon of the illness of the shaman, from which he does not recover "until he begins to shamanize."

> He/she may feel carried off to heaven where he receives instruction from a divinity or from a female figure, an invisible heavenly spouse, a magical anima (1975,

p. 100) or to the underworld where he remains locked up for a time and is often dismembered by the spirits of sufferers of other tortures. The central element is always the same: death and symbolic resurrection. (Eliade, 1964, pp. 5, 56)

With so much uncertainty, such profound disorientation, the ground beneath Jung's feet slipped out from under him. At the age of thirty-eight he claimed in despair that he had "reached a dead end" (Brome, 1981, p. 156).

Shortly after the parting with Freud, and around the start of this "period of inner uncertainty," Jung, who loved to sail, decided to take a cruise on Lake Zurich with several friends. During this four-day stretch on the water, one of these friends took to

reading aloud the *Nekyia* episode of Homer's *Odyssey*, the journey of Ulysses to the Sojourn of the Dead. (Ibid., p. 157)

This episode on Lake Zurich was noteworthy for Jung in that he soon embarked on a period of his life that he likened to his own *Nekyia*, his own journey into the underworld. Images and dreams pounded him with an autonomy that provoked an internal conflict sufficient enough to cause him to step down from his academic position. Von Franz says that "the unconscious has its own ways of revealing what is destined in a human life just at that time when it is ready to be integrated" (Ibid., p. 120). Truly, the unconscious was revealing itself and Jung relinquished himself to the pull of these inner contents, not knowing to what ends they would lead him.

A long period of self-analysis ensued, during which time Jung remained "on ship," albeit no longer its "captain."

Creative play helped to establish some calm but in the long run "something erupted…which I found difficult to control" (Ibid., p. 159). Slowly, the waves of inner tension mounted until he "stood helpless before an alien world." With unceasing intensity, the floodgates let loose, but not without some willingness on Jung's part. In *Memories, Dreams and Reflections*, Jung describes the fateful moment when he committed himself to exploring the unconscious.

> It was during Advent of the year 1913—December 12, to be exact—that I resolved upon the decisive step. I was sitting at my desk once more, thinking over my fears. Then I let myself drop. Suddenly it was as though the ground literally gave way beneath my feet, and I plunged down into dark depths. (1963, p. 179)

Jacob Boehme's defining vision was that of the dark abyss. Jung also initially experienced falling into dark depths. In later episodes he actually made conscious "attempts to get to the very bottom," saying,

> The first time I reached, as it were, a depth of about a thousand feet; the next time I found myself at the edge of a cosmic abyss. It was like a voyage to the moon, or a descent into empty space. First came the image of a crater, and I had the feeling that I was in the land of the dead. (Ibid., p. 181)

He did fear that "there was some psychic imbalance in himself." The vessel, his ego in relation to his psyche, threatened to turn over and go under, straight down into what felt to him like a plummeting into an immeasurable sea. Yet, while all of this may have "capsized" many an ordinary psyche, Jung discovered within himself a strength to endure the torrential undercurrents of the unconscious, a strength that was fueled by a voracious hunger for understanding and was also coupled with "'an unswerving conviction that' he was 'obeying a higher will'" (Brome, p. 159).

Jung did receive unexpected understanding in the form of an inner guide who appeared in one of his dreams. This guide, whom Jung named Philemon, appeared in his dream as a "winged being sailing across the sky." Then he "saw that it was actually an old man with the horns of a bull" and the "wings of the kingfisher with its characteristic colors." The major contribution of the appearances of Philemon to Jung was the "crucial insight that there are things in the psyche that I do not produce, but that produce themselves and have their own life." It was Philemon that taught Jung about "psychic objectivity, the reality of the psyche" (1963, p. 183).

Citing Eliade, von Franz makes a point that relates to Jung's *Nekyia,* emphasizing the role of the shaman in the life of the collective. It is the shaman who

> leads the dead into the "realm of shadows" and serves as mediator between them and their gods;...[he] is the great specialist in the human soul; he alone "sees" it, for he knows its "form and its destiny." (von Franz, 1975, p. 99; Eliade, 1964, p. 8 passim)

Jung was certainly destined to "lead the dead" from the shadows, but first, the dead came to him. They came primarily in the form of dreams, featuring corpses, mummified tombs, and sarcophagi. Attired in the remnants of antique clothing, something clamored for life, for consciousness. Although not related specifically to God for Jung, something willed itself before the eye of consciousness with a tremendous impulse of desire and will, not unlike the will of Boehme's God who is a mystery to himself until God becomes conscious of God's self.

What of the archaic past, of the primordial underworld was trying to "link with the living?" Jung wondered. Reflecting on this period much later in life, he recalled the significance of this inner journey—this *Nekyia*—to the development of his life's work:

> The years when I was pursuing my inner images were the most important in my life—in them everything essential was decided. It all began then; the later details are only supplements and clarifications of the material that burst forth from the unconscious, and at first swamped me. It was the *prima materia* for a lifetime's work. (1963, p. 199)

Notwithstanding the torrent of images and the fear that they produced in him, Jung, very much like Boehme, came to understand that these experiences taught him much of great value. These were lessons he did not learn in a university or medical school. These were lessons he especially did not learn from Freud.

But first, Jung was to endure his *Nekyia* for three more years, six in toto. "Gradually the outlines of an inner change began making their appearance within me" Jung relates. In 1916, three years into his *Nekyia*, he experienced "an urge to give shape to something," an inner compulsion "to formulate and express what might have been said by Philemon" (1963, pp. 189–90). In the "peculiar language" of this outpouring, Jung discovers an analogue between his abyss and the psychological expression of the collective unconscious.

No longer is the abyss merely negative and within the Christian notion. Radically different from the Christian images that Jung had inherited of abyss as hell, devils and death, having experienced first hand some of the oblivion of abyss, it acquires a new name, *Pleroma*, and a twenty-five-page textual amplification, the *Septem Sermones*.

JUNG AND THE PLEROMA

In the following vivid passage from *Memories, Dreams and Reflections*, Jung reveals something of the immediate psychological matrix from which the *Septem Sermones* flowed over "the course of three evenings:"

> It began with a restlessness, but I did not know what it meant or what "they" wanted of me. There was an ominous atmosphere all around me. I had the strange feeling that the air was filled with ghostly entities. Then it was as if my house began to be haunted....
>
> Around five o'clock in the afternoon on Sunday the front doorbell began ringing frantically....The atmosphere was thick, believe me! Then I knew that something had to happen. The whole house was filled as if there were a crowd present, crammed full of spirits. They were packed deep right up to the door, and the air was so thick it was scarcely possible to breathe. As for myself, I was all aquiver with the question: "For God's sake, what in the world is this?" Then they cried out in chorus, "We have come back from Jerusalem where we found not what we sought." (1963, pp. 189–190)

Below I introduce the initial portion of Jung's Myth as revealed in *Septem Sermones ad Mortuos*. I have combined translations from two sources (Robert Segal, *The Gnostic Jung,* as well as Stephen Hoeller, *The Gnostic Jung* and the *Seven Sermons to the Dead)* to suit my goals and purpose. I am considering only the initial segment of the *Sermones, Sermo I,* as well as the last, *Sermo, VII,* as the bookends necessary to illustrate that unitary reality underlies all psychological experience.

Jung's "Gnostic" Myth

I begin with nothingness. Nothingness is the same as fullness. In infinity, fullness is the same as emptiness. Nothingness is both empty and full. We cannot say that this nothingness exists or does not exist. We cannot say that it is nor that it is not. The eternal and infinite possess no qualities nor attributes but it has all qualities. We give qualities and attributes to this Nothingness, but such things are of our thinking and being.

A symbol of this nothingness or fullness is the Pleroma. In the Pleroma there is nothing and everything. Thinking about the Pleroma is fruitless. To do so would mean self-dissolution

The Pleroma is the beginning and the end of the created world. The Pleroma penetrates the Created World completely just as the sunlight penetrates the air. The Created World, however, is not in the Pleroma, but in itself. The Created World is not identical in essence but the essence of the Pleroma is present within us. Created World and Creature are distinguished from the Pleroma. Our essence is limited to time in space. But because the Pleroma is the nothingness which is everywhere complete and without end, we are part of the Pleroma. Think of this allegorically or figuratively. If the Pleroma is everywhere complete, then even in the smallest point of the Created World is a portion of the Pleroma. The Pleroma itself is not divided into parts because it is nothingness. But figuratively speaking, as its parts, the Pleroma, we are also its totality. The Pleroma is at once the smallest, hypothetical even non-existent point within us as it is at the same time the limitlessness of the cosmos about us. Figuratively speaking, in the image of its non-existent point or in the image of its boundless expanse, we are, in image, both its center and its circumference. In the image, we participate in the eternal and infinite.

This image I am giving you all is a beginning, in order to begin somewhere and to say that there is nothing within or without the Created World which is absolutely firm and definite. Everything fixed and certain is relative. The only certainty we have is that the Created World is subject to change. The Pleroma does not change, but we change because we have qualities. (Segal, 1992, pp. 181–193; Hoeller, 1982, pp. 44–58)

The Pleroma, for Jung, describes an uncreated potentiality beyond time and space from which all being emerges. It is a given state of oneness or unity in which all potential opposites comingle in their uncreated state. The image of Pleroma is found in the original Gnostic creation myth, although Jung had not done extensive reading of Gnostic literature until after his *Nekyia* and the writing of *Septem Sermones!*

Historically, the Gnostics existed as an ancient Christian sect in the second century. Their primary doctrine consisted of a belief in the Pleroma as a *place* of primordial unity from which human nature and the universe have fallen. Creation takes place outside the Pleroma (1959a, par. 295), resulting in a dualism of divinity, human beings, and the universe. In sum, for the Gnostics, immateriality is good because matter is evil. The souls of human beings are imprisoned in their bodies. The Gnostics yearned to restore their original unity, which meant to return to an original preexistent, nonmaterial state. They believed that they could effect this restoration only through a special knowledge and the redemption of a savior who would restore the primordial unity of all immateriality (Segal, 1992, p. 3).

Consciously or unconsciously, in expressing the unitary reality he had experienced in his *Nekyia*, Jung had drawn upon the Gnostic creation myth and had used its language and imagery in the writing of his *Septem Sermones*. Only later does Jung explore the Gnostic myth more objectively in terms of the unfolding dualistic nature of the universe. In "A Psychological Approach to the Trinity," Jung relates,

> Inasmuch as the devil was an angel created by God and "fell like lightning from heaven," he, too, is a divine "procession" that became Lord of this world. It is significant that the Gnostics thought of him sometimes as the imperfect demiurge and sometimes as the Saturnine archon, Ialdabaoth. Pictorial representations of this archon correspond in every detail with those of a diabolical demon. He symbolized the power of darkness from which Christ came to rescue humanity. The archons issued from the womb of the unfathomable abyss, i.e., from the same source that produced the Gnostic Christ. (1958, par. 255)

The Gnostics with their fantastic cast of characters (e.g., Ialdabaoth, Abraxas, Achamoth, Sophia, et al.) inspire almost equal trepidation in some quarters as does the notion of Abyss. Linking Jung to the Gnostics has long been used by many to discredit him as a serious psychotheorist and to malign the *Septem Sermones ad Mortuos* for the dualism it implies between Pleroma and Creatura. Martin Buber used Jung's interest in the Gnostics to dismiss the possibility of his having anything relevant to say regarding religion.

Nonetheless, it is doubtful that Jung intended his myth to represent an identical worldview to that of the Gnostics. Many scholars link Jung and Gnosticism based upon his vision in *Septem Sermones*, but Jung was primarily seeking historical sources that would provide evidence for his own experience of the collective unconscious. When he finally came to study Gnosticism, years after his *Nekyia*, he moved on quickly to a study of alchemy that he found to be a more substantial prefiguring of his experience (Segal, p. 8). (For discussions on this subject and for analyses of the *Septem Sermones*, there are many excellent hermeneutical works to be considered (cf. for instance, Robert A. Segal, *The Gnostic Jung;* Stephen A. Hoeller, *The Gnostic Jung and the Seven Sermons to the Dead;* James W. Heisig, *Imago Dei;* Gerhard Wehr, *Jung;* James Olney, *The Rhizome and the Flower;* Gilles Quispel, C. G. *Jung und die Gnosis.*)

It should be stated for clarification that Jung used the language of Gnostic myth, but I reemphasize that he did not even formally study Gnosticism until after his *Nekyia.* Thus, what he is relating in his treatise is his experience, not Gnostic doctrine. Robert Segal's discussion is perhaps most insightful on this issue.

Segal tells us that the essential difference between Jung's Pleroma-Creatura myth and Gnosticism is that Jung's myth is not about the unfolding universe but about the human psyche. For Jung,

> the godhead symbolizes the unconscious. It is the source or agent of everything else. Prior to its emanating anything, it is whole, self-sufficient, perfect. The godhead thus symbolizes the unconscious before the emergence of the ego out of it. It is not that matter pre-exists and emanates out of the godhead but that the ego emerges out of the primordial unconscious. (Ibid., 19–21)

Further, Segal points out that in other Gnostic myths "the unconscious (the dead) is seeking to reveal itself *to* ego consciousness" (the living). In the *Septem Sermones,* the unconscious is seeking revelation *from* ego consciousness. Curiously, this may recall the distinction I made earlier, following Cousins, between kataphatic and apophatic experience and the distinction I made concerning whether or not we are objects that reflect the reflection of the spherical mirror or objects that intersect a plane of the mirror.

Segal continues: other Gnostic myths symbolize the dead,

> "as the state of ego consciousness severed from the unconscious." Jung, in contrast, is addressing the state of undifferentiated unconsciousness itself. The goal remains the raising of unconsciousness to conscious, but now it is the unconscious which is imploring ego consciousness to raise it. (Ibid., p. 39)

Thus, in contrast to Boehme, Jung is not talking about the divine and offering metaphysics, but is offering a psychological explanation for his experience of the abyss that he came to call Pleroma. Boehme on the other hand, as I have shown, and will discuss further in the next chapter, is offering us wisdom about divinity and our relationship to divinity.

In essence, "in the beginning" for Jung is about primordial unconsciousness, undifferentiated nothingness and fullness. His creation myth is about how Creatura and created beings (the ego) develop. Development entails the ego, in relation to the unconscious, sorting out "all the pairs of opposites that are undifferentiated and integrating both sides of all opposites. Integration means balance rather than one-sidedness" (Ibid., pp. 39–40). Thus, the major difference between Jung and the Gnostics would be the fact of making what is unconscious conscious rather than just naming it and relating *to* it as other. The main difference between Jung and Boehme is that Jung is, according to Segal, reducing the godhead to the unconscious. I address this notion further in my final chapter in the context of Jung's concept of *coniunctio* and *unus mundus*.

What is of particular interest here is the symbol that arose from Jung's deep imaginal experience, as well as the nature of the experience itself and the potential value and meaning that the symbol might have for clinical practice in terms of how we might further understand the opposites inherent to the human psyche in light of their mysterious and paradoxical ground.

Interestingly, the abyss/Pleroma of Jung's *Septem Sermones* reverses the image of abyss from an unfathomable, bottomless something in which to fall endlessly, to a preexistence from which all being emerges (1958, par. 255), quite paralleling Boehme's experience of abyss as both nothing and all. The Pleroma is something that exists in our experience that is so profound in its otherness that it feels like this something must be expressed as a Nothing (noting that Nothing, too, is an image; thus, the difficulty inherent to this material).

This mysterious Nothing exists as a harmony of all opposites: emptiness and fullness. To give "qualities" or attributes to this Nothing other than to identify it as a first ground (or un-ground) is impossible. The Pleroma itself is a glimpse of something that feels like it originates beyond the categories of what we know and think.

We cannot remain there long and get only glimpses of this reality through our experience. Yet, the experience of the Pleroma is so radical that we are persuaded that it, this Nothing that is all, is our beginning and our end, as Jung attests.

In contrast to the Pleroma, human nature is of the realm of *Creatura*. We are distinct from the Pleroma, but we are penetrated completely by its essence. The opposites that exist in the Pleroma in harmony exist in us, too, but they exist in us as an unresolved tension.

In distinguishing Creatura from Pleroma, Jung is emphasizing that the purpose of being human is to strive toward the resolution of the opposites within us so that they exist in harmony. Working toward the resolution of opposites fulfills our human goal, which is to be distinct, differentiated, individuated.

The Pleroma is boundless, continuous, and eternal. In contrast, Creatura (including human life and human psyche) are bound in time and space. We partake of the boundlessness of the Pleroma in that we are the parts that make up the whole of the Creatura that, as a totality, is in reflection of the Pleroma. In image, we are both its center and its circumference. If we live in the image, which is to participate in its *totality*—the fullness and emptiness of the Pleroma, which we experience as opposites in us—then we, too, are drawn in to what is eternal and infinite.

This early vision of the Pleroma came as a dramatic explanation of the nature of the origins of the unconscious and consciousness, or we might say the nature of original unity. The divine drama Jung experienced sets forth in powerful imagery the birth of the created world out of a unity that exists in the image of the producer and product, the latter not identical to the former, but similar.

Although Jung, in contrast to Boehme, does not take a definitive theological stance, and although his views may even appear at times to be self-contradictory, he says in one letter, "[m]y human limitation does not permit me to know God," while in a BBC interview he says of God, "I don't need to believe, I know" (Edinger, 1996, p. 124; BBC interview, *Face to Face*, Oct. 22, 1959, quoted in Edinger, p. 137). Jung would say that the Pleroma is primarily a psychological expression of numinous experience. This psychological experience is, for him, a legitimate expression of a symbol equally valid in integrity to other numinous expressions of the godhead (1959b, p. 209).

Suffice it to say that for Jung these initial visions were the ground (un-ground) for all of his subsequently formed ideas about analytical psychology and the nature of the psyche. As Jung says, toward the end of his life,

> All my works, all my creative activity, has come from those initial fantasies and dreams which began in 1912, almost fifty years ago. Everything that I

accomplished in later life was already contained in them, although at first only in the form of emotions and images. (1963, p. 192)

Likewise, Boehme spends the rest of his years writing about his experience of the *Ungrund*, and what emerges from it, the Eternal Idea, or Sophia. It is clear that Boehme and Jung encountered these respective realities at a point of major life transition and psychic turmoil. Their encounters of radical otherness grounded them anew in a specific reality that was dynamic and arresting enough that they maintained a lifelong relationship with this mysterious ground.

I will now proceed to explore further the nature of the "event" of these experiences, an unfolding process of the *Ungrund* and Pleroma, and to discuss what I believe to be a unitary reality underlying all psychological experience. This unitary reality, once experienced, is often profound enough to turn our lives around in a quite different direction from where we were headed.

5

When Deep Calls unto Deep

As a hart longs for flowing streams,
so longs my heart for Thee, O God. (Psalm 42:1)

I N THE PREVIOUS two chapters I have related how Jacob Boehme and Carl Jung were each profoundly moved by what I have identified, following Neumann, deep experiences of a unitary reality. The parallels in their lives, which led to these experiences as well as their individual responses to them, are many. For example, in responding to the pull of a strong inner call, each had to "swim against the tide" of his own world. Individual "mystical" experience leading to claims of personal revelation was discouraged or disregarded in the "enlightened" Protestant and scientific circles of these men; nonetheless, each was attuned to the inexorable tug of his own inner journey. Each was led into this unknown territory by a series of profound visions.

Although these visions may have followed a disintegrating period of melancholy or psychic disturbance, in the end, they led to healing rather than further disintegration for each. These were humbling, not inflationary, experiences, which left each with a feeling of awe and gratitude. Finally, these experiences led both Boehme and Jung to the production of a voluminous body of written work that touched the imagination of multitudes of contemporaries and continues to inspire successors.

In this chapter, I first examine the nature of these experiences as they have been communicated to us in their own words and in those of others. Then, I will analyze the experiences from the point of view of depth psychology and religion. Finally, I will begin to draw lessons from these experiences for clinical practice.

Nature of the Experience

What did Boehme and Jung experience? Can we identify and name distinguishing marks that are unique to the nature and experience of this reality?

I believe it is possible to recognize at least five distinct traits related to the experience of unitary reality, as observed in both Boehme and Jung, and as we will see in other examples to follow. This experience of unitary reality:

1. Is a dynamic process in which the content of the experience is vital
2. Begins with a period of confusion, melancholy, and/or psychic suffering
3. Involves a journey into an extraordinary "inner space"
4. Leads to further integration of the personality
5. Inspires a feeling of awe and gratitude

We can see how these five traits will illuminate the abyss/unitary reality.

I. A VITAL AND DYNAMIC PROCESS

The *Ungrund* for Boehme may be a no-thingness, but it is not static. A clue is given us in the dynamic language Boehme uses to describe the vitality of the experience of unitary reality for him. He says in a letter to a friend, for example, that "the gate was *opened* unto me" (Waterfield, 1989, p. 63). In *Aurora* he confides that his "spirit *directly saw* through all things" (1915, xix, 13). Martensen explains that the original vision that arose from the light shining on the pewter dish produced in Boehme an "inward ecstasy" (Martensen, 1949, p. 5).

Further describing the effect of the experience upon him, Boehme says "the fire burning within me is driving me on," causing his hand and pen to "follow the thoughts as well as they can." Mixing metaphors he equates the inspiration to a "shower of rain" (Alleman, 1932, p. 28).

Nicolas Berdyaev, who developed a philosophy of freedom and the creative act founded upon the notion of dynamic tension in Boehme's *Ungrund*, speaks of it as a "primal source and fount of being from which an eternal torrent pours" (1936, pp. 54–55). The *Ungrund* is the fullness of everything existing in potentiality and the ultimate source of every manifestation. Through the *Ungrund* we are connected to freedom as pure possibility, to the groundless "ground" of being in the preexistential abyss (McLachlan, 1992, p. 140), to "the unfathomable irrationality of freedom in pure possibility, in the forces concealed within that dark void that precedes all positive determination of being" (Berdyaev, 1935, p. 165). Spirit is associated with a dynamic transcendent. Wheras this describes Boehme's revelation more than the experience itself, and is once removed from the source, Berdyaev has the image right: that of an eternally dynamic and flowing fountain from pre-being into being.

Boehme's *Ungrund*, then, is clearly not the locus of a static and uneventful "nothingness." His are dynamic and vital images of burning fire, showers of rain, the will of God smashing "the earthly formation of the rational will" (1978, p. 209).

Like Boehme, Jung's experience of unitary reality was similarly vital and dynamic. The images that "burst forth from the unconscious, and at first swamped" him, were alive with power and potential (1963, p. 199). The culmination of experiences and images inspired him to go to great ends, even when censored, to record and amplify in detail the contents of his visions.

The words Jung chooses to describe the backdrop for the writing of *Septem Sermones* are likewise vibrant and teeming with presence. As he describes it in his memoirs, the house was "filled as if there were a crowd present, crammed full of spirits" (Ibid., pp. 189–90).

Jung's introduction to his "inner guide" was equally vivid. Philemon first appears to Jung in a dream as a fantastic "being sailing across the sky" on the "wings of the kingfisher with its characteristic colors" (Ibid., p. 183). And what Philemon reveals to Jung, "that there are things in the psyche which I do not produce, but which produce themselves" (Ibid.), is a lesson of the fact and vitality of the unconscious, a lesson revealed to Jung only through his journey into it.

2. BEGINS WITH A PERIOD OF CONFUSION, MELANCHOLY, AND/OR PSYCHIC SUFFERING

As both Edinger (1995, pp. 24–25) and von Franz (1975, p.120) have said, the one who journeys to the under-world—whether the journey of a "hero" or a "sha-man"—begins the trip after a period of disorientation, fragmentation, or illness. The place to which they are journeying is a place that is either beyond all opposites or contains them in balance. The place from which they are departing manifests the tension of opposing forces at war.

This was certainly true in the case of Boehme and Jung. As we have already seen, Boehme relates this in *Aurora:* "at last I fell into a very deep melancholy and heavy sad-ness, when I beheld and contemplated the great deep of this world" (1915, p. 485). Jung had just made the break from Freud, his mentor, friend, and sponsor in the con-text of their differences over the subject of sexuality and the relationship of sexuality to psychic wholeness (1963, p. 168). Beyond its personal significance and its biologi-cal function, Jung's primary concern was to investigate the spiritual aspect and numinous meaning of sexuality espe-cially in terms of chthonic spirit, or what he called "the dark side of the God-image" (Ibid. 1989, par. 634 ff). He referred to this time as "a period of inner uncertainty" and had the feeling that he was "totally suspended in mid-air" (1963, p. 170). There is a factor of stress, external and/or internal, which either simmers to a boiling point, or that is ignored or remains out of the ego's reach. The ego is up against something other than its own world orientation. I have shown some indication of these factors at work in the examples of Boehme and Jung in chapters four and five.

To re-create the exact personal and historical situation of either is impossible. These two had the experiences, and everything that I might speculate upon is secondary to the experience itself. What we can see in both of these and other examples, however, is that there is purpose to the suffering. Something changes that needs to change.

3. Involves a journey into an extraordinary "inner space"

In the preceding two chapters, I have discussed the descent of Boehme and Jung into a deep inner world. They may speak of that world in a different language, but its geography is strikingly similar. Above all, they share an experience of unitary reality. For Boehme, the *Ungrund* is perceived as an eternal truth early in the journey. There was little in Boehme's Lutheran tradition that could have prepared him for the immediate encounter with such a radically other *otherness*. This preexistent state is the place from which a *theogenesis* occurs. *Theogenesis* refers to the process in which God emerges and is made distinct from the *Ungrund*, which he did not create (McLachlan, 1992, p. 138). In Boehme's vision, it is God himself who is brought into being from pre-being. This theogonic complement to the story of the creation of the cosmos is a direct result of Boehme's attending to his inner journey.

Boehme also saw things in his descent that were alarming. His inner journey was not all the peaceful and blissful state of "Liberty" blue (liberty pertaining to the *Ungrund*), the revelation of light (Aurora, dawn), and "spirit of the

Fire-flash" (the tranforming quality of spirit). Indeed, he discovered the *dark nature of God*, which is filled with wrathfire, devils, hell, and judgment (cf. Boehme, 1915, chapters 9, 17, 19 passim). The dark nature of God was translated into numerous images that sought to display what he encountered there, such as an eternally burning fire, the bitter quality of heat or fire without light, "the darkness of the love-*ens*," or paradisical light, being shut up in death as an austere, dark source of pain, horror, torment, and disquietude. These images reveal a complex and intricate world that opened itself to him. It was Boehme's experience of unitary reality that was able to hold the opposites of a God of goodness and a God of wrathfire and judgment.

Jung references the Pleroma during the *Septem Sermones*, three years into his *Nekyia*. I would argue, however, that his six-year inner journey was replete with *pleromatic experience*, and it was in the *Septem Sermones* that he gave it a name. Jung's *Nekyia* was populated with singular characters. In a vivid example, he relates that, in one early fantasy, Elijah and Salome appeared to him along with a "black serpent living with them which displayed an unmistakable fondness for me" (1963, p. 181), Philemon swooping in with the wings of a kingfisher and "walking up and down the garden" with Jung, as if Philemon were a "guru" (Ibid., p. 183).

In his biography of Jung, V. Brome says that Jung took the precarious but brave route, eschewed by most people, in his descent into this inner world. "The unconscious was charged with infinite potential, but modern man considered it too dangerous to entrust himself to the hazardous paths, haunted by demons capable of human embodiment, which led into its more profound depths" (Brome, 1981, p. 164).

Boehme was inspired to compose works that have also inspired many who followed him, among these, Carl Jung who cites Boehme in twelve volumes of the *Collected Works* in fifty-five different instances. Clearly Jung was taken by the investigations of Boehme into the "abyss of darkness" (1959a, par. 555). Jung endorsed Boehme highly saying,

"It seems to me of paramount importance that Protestantism should integrate psychological experience, as for instance [Jacob Boehme] did" (1954, par. 1654). Like Boehme, Jung voluntarily took the plunge into the depths—at times on the brink of madness—and it was this hero's journey, this shaman's descent, which revealed to him "the *prima materia* for [his] lifetime's work" (1963, p. 199).

4. Leads to further integration of the personality

Boehme talked of a "triumphing of the spirit" following his experiences, and compared the consequent feeling of liberation to a "resurrection from the dead" (1915, p. 488). He also writes of a process of the spirit entering the body and creating wholeness in a seventeenth-century statement of what Jung would call *individuation*. He says that "life then went forth from God's speaking, and came into the body, and is nothing other than the formed will of God." This is followed by the admonition to still one's own "self-image and willing" so that "divine forming and will will rise up" (1978, p. 209).

Although written in the language of religion, these are images of psychic healing and integration that come only after a relinquishing of the precious defenses and projections of the ego. It is the movement from a smaller "I" to a larger "I," an "I" that embodies the very will of God. It is Boehme's restatement of St. Paul when he says, "I have been crucified with Christ; it is no longer I who live, but Christ who lives in me" (*Holy Bible*, Gal. 2:20, p. 212).

We know that Jung's breakdown and journey into the unconscious led to a breakthrough and a healing. We know this since the evidence that Jung led a highly productive and creative life is vast. Rather than a succumbing into dissolution and madness, as Nietzsche's descent led him, Jung's voyage was a true *Nekyia*, a hero's journey, from which the traveler returns with deeds accomplished and tales to tell.

Marie Louise von Franz tells us that Jung could have chosen to go the route of a shaman, but he elected rather to travel the path of an empirical scientist. He may have hidden away some of his most intimate thoughts in the *Septem Sermones*, which was not intended for publication but ultimately was released, and the *Red Book*, which is now in publication under the editorship of Jung historian, Sonu Shamdasani, who will bring this unpublished work to the public by 2009 through the support of the Philemon Foundation. The images that he encountered during his six-year inner journey, and his interrelationship with them, however, were directly responsible for some of the most profound theories on the life of the human psyche.

5. Inspires a Feeling of Awe and Gratitude

Von Franz has said that our finite life has meaning only when it is related to the infinite through the "window on eternity" (1975, p. 250). Boehme was so grateful to have relief from his gloomy melancholy that he found it hard to communicate, either in speaking or in writing, this "triumphing of the spirit" as he called it (1915, p. 488). At having the "gate opened" to him and being granted a direct vision into the eternal truths, he later said in a letter to a friend "thereupon I turned my heart to praise God for it" (Waterfield, 1989, p. 64).

Jung speaks to the meaning of our "finite life" many years later in *Memories, Dreams and Reflections*:

> Only if we know that the thing which truly matters is the infinite can we avoid fixing our interest upon futilities, and upon all kinds of goals which are not of real importance....If we understand and feel that here in this life we already have a link with the infinite, desires and attitudes change. In the final analysis, we count for something only because of the essential we embody, and if we do not embody that, life is wasted. In our relationships to other men, too, the crucial question is whether an element of boundlessness is expressed in the relationship. (1963, p. 325)

In such an experience of unitary reality, Boehme, Jung, and we with Boehme and Jung, come to know that we have personal identity and that our identity extends beyond the life of the ego. We are not ultimately like the drop of water poised above the ocean, losing all attributes, as we plunge in. We are distinct selves and personalities.

It is this glimpse through the "window of eternity" that inspires awe and gratitude.

I now turn to an analysis of the experience of unitary reality from the viewpoint of depth psychology and religion. In this analysis, I draw from the works of von Franz, Erich Neumann, Edward Edinger, Ann Belford Ulanov, Tomás Agosin, and Nicolas Berdyaev, as well as the writings of Jacob Boehme and Carl Jung.

ANALYSIS OF THE EXPERIENCE

Marie-Louise Von Franz is helpful to our understanding as she correlates the experience of unitary reality, which we see in both Boehme and Jung, with a period of great suffering. At some point, they reach a pit of darkness. Yet, it is different from the immobilization of clinical depression, or total breakdown, more, perhaps, like the spiritual "dark night" of Saint John of the Cross. Both Boehme and Jung were functional. Boehme continued his cobbler's business. Jung continued his practice, albeit at times he found that he had to keep reminding himself who he was, what he did, and where he lived (1963, p. 189).

Erich Neumann helps us by distinguishing between the suffering of the ego and its dissolution. The former often precedes the experience of unitary reality, while the latter is more likely a precursor to psychosis. In his volume *The Place of Creation*, Neumann tells us that,

> [d]ecreased consciousness with a dissolving ego, as seen in pathological cases, does not bring about an experience of the unitary world of the archetypal field....But whenever this ego, though changed (for instance, through deep emotions) is not dissolved, an

experience of the unitary world takes place that is
an expansion of world knowledge in which the conscious mind participates as well. (Neumann, 1989,
pp. 54–55)

Neumann answers our unspoken questions about
Boehme and Jung, or anyone for that matter that makes
claims of personal revelation through inner visions, dreams,
and "voices." Are these true? How can we distinguish the
difference between a mystical, or deeply spiritual experience, and that of psychosis?

VISIONS OR DELUSIONS?

As clinicians, we must be able to discern whether a patient's
inner visions are indications of an experience of unitary reality or evidence of madness, and we should not be so quick to
collapse one into the other. As a result of two contempora-
neous events—one a real-life drama, and the other a movie
based upon a real-life drama—the face of schizophrenia
has finally been accorded cover-story status at *Newsweek*
magazine (Begley, 2002). A mother had been put on trial
for causing the horrific drowning deaths of her five children.
Her defense was that insistent inner voices told her that the
children needed to die in order to be "saved," voices that
could be quelled only by injections of the powerful, antipsy-
chotic drug, Haldol. A tough, Texas jury ignored her insanity
defense and, despite the protestations of her defense counsel
that her doctor had just two weeks prior taken her off Haldol,
convicted her of second degree murder. The other example
mentioned by the magazine was that of Dr. John Nash, a
Princeton mathematician, and subject of a popular book and

Oscar-winning film, both by the name of *A Beautiful Mind*, who was plagued by inner voices of schizophrenia, but who also won the Nobel Prize.

Roberto Tomás Agosin, the late psychiatrist and former Associate Director of Residency Training and Assistant Clinical Professor of Psychiatry at Albert Einstein College of Medicine and founder of the Psychotherapy and the Spirit Seminars at the Cafh Foundation, New York, has given us a valuable map to help us discern whether the experience of what we are calling *unitary reality* bears the marks of psychosis or of mysticism.

Even though as clinicians we may not be directly concerned with mysticism or mystical practice, I do feel that the qualifications made by Agosin are helpful in understanding the nature of the experience of unitary reality as I am approaching it as one in which the ego can navigate in relation to radical other otherness in contrast to becoming swamped or flooded by it. He prefaces his discussion "Psychosis, Dreams, and Mysticism in the Clinical Domain" with the statement that, for the clinician,

> to speak of God, the Divine, the sacred, the awesome, can be considered breaking the boundaries of clinical work. It is the realm of the religious and not the consulting room. But I have found that the spiritual realm and the divine cannot be left outside of the clinician's concern. (Agosin, 1992, pp. 41–42)

And how can it be? If, as I contend, a unitary reality underlies all psychological experience, then as clinicians we ignore the "spiritual realm and the divine" at the risk of the total psychic health of those in our care. The "spiritual realm" is the matrix from which emerges personality and identity. Whether it is, in the end, an overwhelming and dissolving experience, or one that is awakening and enlivening, depends upon the ability of the ego to receive and house it.

As Von Franz tells us, there is no human life in which an experience of this unitary reality does not break through at least once (von Franz, 1994, p. 337). This being the case, it is important that, as clinicians, we are alert to the dynamics of the experience, and are able to distinguish it from the disintegrating experience of ego dissolution.

Nonetheless, Agosin says that this discernment is not an easy thing to do. It is confusing primarily because, as Agosin has found through a comparative analysis, there are many similarities between the experiences of psychosis and mysticism (Agosin, pp. 49–52). To the observer, the experiences of mysticism and psychosis may look the same upon initial observation. There are also a number of significant differences. The differences become the determining clues as to whether the subject is having a mystical experience or exhibiting psychotic symptoms.

As we examine the reported experiences of Jacob Boehme and Carl Jung, we first see that they share a number of the similarities that Agosin has discovered. The first relevant similarity observed between mystical experience and psychosis is that of an "intense subjective experience." There is no question but that both Boehme's and Jung's experience was subjective and intense. They were both "totally focused inwardly" with their attentions shifting "from the external world to the inner life" (Ibid., p. 49).

The second similarity listed by Agosin is a sense of *noesis*, of the reported gaining of new knowledge. The experiences in question were characterized by Boehme and Jung as noetic, including as they did "states of insight into depths of truth unplumbed by the discursive intellect" (Ibid., p. 49). The "unlettered" Boehme strongly felt that he had learned more in fifteen minutes of insight than if he had gone to university. He described this in *Aurora*.

> *From this light now it is that I have my knowledge*, as also my *will, impulse and driving*, and therefore I will set down this knowledge in writing according to my gift, and let God work his will; and though I should *irritate* or enrage the whole world, the devil, and all the gates of hell, I will look on and wait what the LORD, intendeth with it. (1915, p. 489)

Jung received insights from his inner guide, Philemon, that he had learned from nowhere else. Jung's major theories were at least conceived during the time when he "was pursuing [his] inner images," the period of his journey into the unconscious.

Thirdly, there is a shared ineffable quality to the described experiences of mystics and psychotics. Boehme did not even begin to write of his experiences for twelve years after his vision of light on the pewter dish. As he tells us in *Aurora*, the text he first wrote after the twelve-year lapse,

> Because I could not at once apprehend the *deepest* births of God in their *being*, and comprehend them in my *reason*, there passed almost *twelve* years, before the exact understanding thereof was given me. (1915, p. 489)

Jung became increasingly incoherent and subsequently withdrew from the world of academia and from his social life, and retired to his garden and home. According to his biographer, "[t]he written record of his breakdown and simultaneous self-analysis is rambling, perhaps for this reason it conveys most vividly the almost incoherent upsurge of potentially destructive material" (Brome, 1981, p. 166). Indeed, it was only after Jung picked up the pen to write the *Septem Sermones*, that "the spirits which had invaded the house vanished, and he wrote obsessionally over the course of three evenings. This reawakened expressiveness was symbolic of the "purging of his near-madness" and the "collective unconscious had at last been assimilated in a new harmony" (Ibid., p. 167).

The fourth shared characteristic revealed by Agosin is that of a loss of ego boundaries, leading to a "sense of oneness with others, nature, the universe as a whole" (Agosin, 1992, p. 50). Both Boehme and Jung experienced a temporary loss of ego boundaries especially at the beginning of their visions that loss, I have argued earlier, may have actually served as a catalyst for the experiences of each. We see this clearly in Boehme's description of his early vision.

> In this light my spirit suddenly saw through all, and *in* and *by* all creatures, even in herbs and grass it knew God, who he is, and how he is, and what his will is: And suddenly in that light my will was set on by a mighty *impulse*, to describe *the being of God*. (1915, p. 488)

We see this phenomenon also in Jung's reporting of this period in his memoirs. His is not so much a feeling of merging with nature, but of all consciousness. He is awakened to the collective unconscious, the objective psyche, in these dreams and visions, and begins to understand that he is part of something much larger, something for which his professional education and experience had not prepared him.

> When I look back upon it all today and consider what happened to me during the period of my work on the fantasies, it seems as though a message had come to me with overwhelming force. There were things in the images which concerned not only myself but many others also. It was then that *I ceased to belong to myself alone* [emphasis mine], ceased to have the right to do so. From then on, my life belonged to the generality. (1963, p. 192)

He began to see himself connected on a very deep level with all humanity through images in dreams, symbols, and his understanding of mythology. He began to transcribe these fantasies, accompanied by drawings of mandalas (images of wholeness) and other images in the *Red Book*.

Agosin reveals other similarities between psychosis and mysticism, including perceptual changes, intense affect, and altered states of consciousness. Boehme's seeing through pewter dishes and herbs into the eternal truths of nature and God is a prime example of this. Hans Martensen said that Boehme "fell into an inward ecstasy" at the prospect of gazing "into the very heart of things" (Martensen, 1949, p. 5). Jung's visions of Philemon and his experiencing spirits teeming in his house one beautiful summer day are other examples of this.

The final similarity raised by Agosin is an attempt through the psychosis or mystical experience to achieve renewal, transformation, and healing. The inner journeys of each appeared to be just such attempts of the psyche following difficult periods of melancholy and suffering.

In addition to a host of similarities between psychosis and mystical experience, Agosin recognized a number of differences between them. These distinctions help us to discern more clearly what is really going on in the inner life of the subject. Sometimes it is the one. Sometimes it is the other. Sometimes it is both. These differences relate to such things as self image; the shedding of ego identity; increased serenity; a welcome attitude toward change; no disruption of thought processes; few, if any, aggressive or paranoid elements; visual hallucinatory experience in mysticism; and auditory hallucinations in psychotics, self-limited mystical experience, and the consequence of the experience.

Agosin says that whereas it is true, on the one hand, that mystics "generally seek to reduce their sense of self to a minimum," on the other hand, they also "rejoice in the beauty of God and all its manifestations, which are perceived as wondrous and extraordinary" (Agosin, 1992, p. 53). They do not seek inflation, nor are they long deluded by it.

One of the other clear marks of distinction between psychosis and mystical experience has to do with what Agosin has characterized as a welcome attitude toward change. Not only did Boehme and Jung have such a welcome attitude, but they even precipitated change through their pioneering writings. They bucked the tide of their respective worlds to articulate faithfully what they each discovered in their experiences of unitary reality.

It would appear that Boehme typifies more than Jung does Agosin's characteristic of no-disruption-of-thought processes. Even though in the end Jung's six-year journey into the unconscious was productive, it was also, at the time it was happening, replete with incoherence. There may possibly have been paranoid elements present. According to Brome, "Jung's reminiscences frankly admit how near he came at this period to madness" (1981, p. 166). This tendency is not immediately discernible in Boehme's writings, however, nor in contemporary reports of his behavior.

Both Boehme and Jung had the visual hallucinatory experience characteristic of mysticism. Images abound in writings from the periods in question: Boehme's of the *Ungrund*, of Sophia; Jung's of the Pleroma, of Philemon; and other characters who peopled his dreams and fantasies. Jung, unlike Boehme, did talk of hearing voices, though. Brome, in his biography tells us more of Jung's encounters with Philemon, saying that he,

> walked up and down the garden talking with him, and such a scene in anyone else would certainly have conveyed the impression of a madman listening to his voices. (Ibid., p. 165)

Of course, anyone who has studied acting with a sturdy master teacher or who has practiced any of the other arts or fields of study that involve inner dialogue will know that we are encouraged to talk openly to our inner selves, the inner content of the imaginal becoming evermore real, deeply layered, and enfleshed as we converse these layers into being. Whether these voices were inwardly real and audible or outwardly real and audible for Jung, it is difficult to discern.

The experiences of both Boehme and Jung fit the self-limited category, they lasted a "relatively short time," especially those of Boehme, and displayed a "profound impact on the person who goes through" them. Psychosis, as Agosin says, is more often "a chronic condition, causing great pain and suffering for the individual and others" (1992, p. 54).

In the end, the consequence or the "result" of the experience is the final determinant as to whether it is of mysticism or madness. The true "mystical experience leaves the individual more connected and involved with the world" (Ibid., p. 54).

The clear demarcation between psychosis and mystical experience in our examples of Boehme and Jung can be seen in the fact that each man emerged from his own "journey" with greater wisdom, insight, and generativity than before. Each was transformed into a new man, leader, and guide for those on the path of inner spiritual journeying and individuation.

Jung was painted with the "psychosis brush" by some of his critics. At times, he even believed he was headed there. The final consequence or result of the experience, in Agosin's words, is what assures us that however deep Jung's exploration of the abyssal seas of the psyche took him, he was safely deposited back "on shore." The result of the experience was not disintegration of the personality but the acquisition of new knowledge. This gnosis was integrated into his work and made him the center of a circle of inquirers into the realms of the archetypal layer of the psyche.

In the end, Jung's "breakdown" was a "breakthrough," a creative illness from which emerged a new man. Brome says Jung took the precarious but brave route in his descent into this inner world.

The unconscious was charged with infinite potential, but modern man considered it too dangerous to entrust himself to the hazardous paths, haunted by demons capable of human embodiment, which led into its more profound depths." (Brome, p. 164)

What, then, can we learn from applying Agosin's analytical map to the experiences of Boehme, Jung, and others? One thing, which becomes apparent as we do, is that there is a continuum between psychosis and mysticism. There appear to be both overlapping and divergent characteristics. Even the divergent characteristics are divergent only in degree. One possible explanation I would offer to address this incongruity is that there is one unitary reality that is encountered in mystical and psychotic experience alike. One experiencing the former can house and integrate the encounter, whereas the latter cannot and is, instead, overwhelmed and disintegrated by it.

6

THE SELF: UNITING OPPOSITES

WHAT IS THE map we see here from the lens of analytical psychology? I am talking about an experience of unitary reality that von Franz and others refer to as the field of the Self, or simply the Self-Field. Ann Ulanov speaks of the Self as an "ordering force in the unconscious," saying,

> The Self exists in us as a predisposition to be oriented around a center. It is the archetype of the center, a primordial image similar to images that have fascinated disparate societies throughout history. It is, like all the archetypes, part of the deepest layers of our unconscious which Jung calls "collective" or "objective" to indicate that they exceed our personal experience. We experience the Self existing within our subjectivity, but it is not our property, nor have we originated it; it possesses its own independent life. (Young-Eisendrath and Dawson, 1997, p. 298)

The Self is an archetype that unites oppositions, one that, according to Ulanov, "orders our whole psyche." When we enter into an experience of unitary reality, or when we "cooperate with the approaches of the Self, it feels as if we are connecting with a process of centering, not only for our deepest self, but also for something that extends well beyond our psyche into the center of reality" (Ibid., p. 299).

Neumann seems to echo this when he tells us that the field of the Self is beyond, or a "regulatory field superior to," the archetypal field (Neumann, 1989, p. 20). In describing the stages of ego consciousness in relation to the archetypal field and to the Self-field, Neumann notes that we find at a certain layer of reality a unitary reality existing beyond and before the primal split (consciousness from unconsciousness) that inevitably occurs in which our conscious minds develop into a polarized reality. Except in cases of severe trauma or developmental injury, he believes that most of us have experienced this unitary reality, in some form, while we were in the mother's womb or at a very early stage of development:

> The prenatal egoless totality is associated with an unconscious experience—which can, however, be recalled in later life as a dim memory—of an acosmic state of the world. In this totality there exists a pre-psychic "nebular state" in which there is no opposition between the ego and the world, I and Thou, or the ego and the self. This state of diffusion of the world soul and the corresponding emptiness of the world is *a borderline experience of the beginning of all things which corresponds to the mystic's experience of the universal diffusion of the unitary reality [emphasis mine]*. (Neumann, 1989, p. 74)

Neumann believes that in the case of the mystic's experience, too, the dissolution and overcoming of the ego results in what he is calling a borderline experience (to be distinguished from the *DSM* diagnostic category, "borderline psychosis")—that of absolute knowledge of "the pleromatic phase" meaning the prenatal egoless totality to which I have referred earlier as a sort of preexistence *in utero* in which the ego is not yet incarnate and yet has a psychic reality or awareness.

With the term *absolute knowledge*, Neumann (1975, pp. 79–81) is drawing from Jung (1960, par. 947) and is referring to the Self-field, which contains the knowledge of the archetypes but in its uroboric or undifferentiated form. The symbol of the uroboros—a "serpent coiled into a circle biting its own tail"—represents "a primal state involving darkness and self-destruction as well as fecundity and potential creativity. It portrays the stage that exists before delineation and separation of the opposites" (Samuels, Shorter & Plaut, 1986, p. 158).

Absolute knowledge as Neumann explains it is felt by the pre-ego to be a diffuse feeling of the world and an extension to the limits of the world of an existence no longer enclosed in the body, and in time and space. Then, as the ego develops to become an ego, what was originally an indefinite uroboric unity of the unconscious with all the opposites contained within itself—a Pleromatic unity—this acosmic emptiness and fullness of the psychic dimension disappears. The body scheme of the growing infant is coordinated with the consolidation and differentiation of the ego and the ego begins to replace the once diffuse world with a configured one of precisely demarcated objects. When we are entirely "incorporated" and identical with our egos, we come to live at a fixed place and a clearly defined moment of time. A number of processes can disrupt what Neumann is calling our incorporated self—trauma, intoxication, ecstasy, illness, fatigue, any of these can remove us from our spatial-temporal definiteness (1975, pp. 80–81).

Thus, for Neumann, the Self-field is a preexisting unitary reality from which we emerge. Before we become an ego, we are of this uroboric realm. The field is superior to the archetypal realm. We have known it once, and in mystical experience or some experiences of breakdown, we might experience it again. Neumann is helpful in understanding the experience itself although he limits the experience to a purely psychological ground. At least he is open to diverse forms of experience:

> We are only just beginning to recognize that different psychic constellations are associated with different experiences of the world, and that the world experience associated with our ego-consciousness is only *one* form, and not necessarily the one that is most comprehensive and closest to reality. (Neumann, 1989, pp. 9–10)

From Neumann, we feel as if there is an inheritance that is specifically ours, psychologically so. The pleromatic experience of unitary reality is the beginning, a first ground, a birthright, something that is there from our inception. Developmental injuries and specific traumas may impair an individual's knowledge of this unitary reality, but for Neumann, unitary reality underlies all experience.

With his concept of the psychoid layer, Jung helps us to see beyond our purely psychological beginnings, telling us that he has

> even hazarded the postulate that the phenomenon of archetypal configurations—which are psychic events *par excellence*—may be founded upon a *psychoid* base, that is, upon an only partially psychic

and possibly altogether different form of being. (1963, p. 351)

This would seem to mean that, even though we experience something psychically, what we experience may actually have its origin in a "place" beyond our psychic and psychological modes of apprehension. There is, then, an intersection in the archetype in general, and more specifically in the archetype of the Self, wherein is brought together and held in tension all opposites and "otherness"—wholly, holy, and radically other. The Self archetype would appear to be open at both ends, like the cigar-shaped MRI of my earlier analogy. This see-through place of intersection would be the locus of our encounter with the *Ungrund*/Pleroma.

Jung goes on to say, however, that "[f]or lack of empirical data I have neither knowledge nor understanding of such forms of being, which are commonly called spiritual" (Ibid., p. 351). Such a statement appears to be in direct contradiction to Jung's early experiences "of such forms of being," which I am considering in this book. Has he overlooked here his experiences of the Pleroma, of his *Nekyia*, his night-sea journey into the depths of the unconscious? It would seem so.

Perhaps understanding can be aided by the following statement taken from the same paragraph in his memoirs:

All comprehension and all that is comprehended is in itself psychic, and to that extent we are hopelessly cooped up in an exclusively psychic world. Nevertheless, we have good reason to suppose that behind this veil there exists the uncomprehended absolute object which affects and influences us—and to suppose it even, or particularly, in the case of psychic phenomena about which no verifiable statements can be made. Statements concerning possibility or impossibility are valid only in specialized fields; outside those fields they are merely arrogant presumptions. (Ibid., p. 352)

Here we find Jung offering the disclaimer that he is not a theologian and does not wish to step outside his own "specialized field" to risk being accused of "arrogant presumptions," which is fair enough. However, we also see that he is not foreclosing on the possibility of there being another reality "behind this veil," a reality that may be perceived only on this side of the veil through an "exclusively psychic" perception.

Again, his lack of reference in this discussion to his experience of the Pleroma and the deeper layers of the unconscious, what I have been calling his encounter with unitary reality, is puzzling. There would seem to be only three possible explanations for this: 1) they no longer carried the charge for him in his eighties as they did when he was a young man in his thirties; 2) he considered them illusions; or 3) he did not want to call attention to the fact that he, a scientist, had actually had at best, mystical, and at worst, psychotic, experiences.

Despite how Jung may have characterized or disregarded these experiences in some of his writings and other communications, when viewed in conjunction with those of Boehme and others, it is possible to see, as I have been postulating, clear marks of an encounter with unitary reality that is experienced psychologically but not limited to the psychological.

Jung's self-contradictions can be puzzling and frustrating. Yet there is enough evidence in some of these statements that leans me away from Robert Segal's assertion, referenced in the previous chapter, that Jung reduces the godhead to the unconscious. Here are Segal's words, which presumably represent his characterization of Jung's thought on the subject:

> The godhead symbolizes the unconscious. As a symbol of the unconscious, it is primordial. It is the source or agent of everything else. Prior to its emanating anything, it is whole, self-sufficient, perfect. The godhead thus symbolizes the unconscious before the emergence of the ego out of it. (Segal, 1992, pp. 19–20)

One can even begin to delight in steering the course between the apparent contradictions in Jung's statements to this effect. For instance, in reply to Martin Buber's attacks, Jung claims without hesitation that, "I start from the *facts* for which I seek an interpretation" (1954, par. 1513).

And, at the same time, in another text referencing Yahweh's creation of the world from the void, he states,

> I do not imply any limitation of his omnipotence; on the contrary, it is an acknowledgment that all possibilities are contained in him, and that there are in consequence no other possibilities than those which express him. (1958, par. 630)

Further, even though his encounter may have tread on the turfs of both mystical and psychotic experience, it was, in the final analysis, an experience of unitary reality.

IMAGES OF SOPHIA:
DIVINE MIRROR AND "FIRST EVENT"

Boehme may have been accused of being delusional and even a drunk, but these were only attempts at discrediting him for his original and provocative writings that put him, some said, at serious odds with orthodox Christian theology. Primarius Richter, of Boehme's church in Görlitz, proclaimed publicly that Boehme was,

> fuddled every day with brandy, as well as beer and other liquor, and was a rogue and vagabond; "all which," adds Boehme, "is untrue, and he himself is a drunken man." In short, "[Richter] raged violently against the printed book, as if his son had been murdered and all his goods burned, and poured out a heap of lies against me, along with wanton defamation." (Boehme, 1930, p. liii)

Despite these feeble accusations, Boehme's were classic mystical visions, which Agosin's map helps us to see more clearly. What does this analysis say about Boehme's experiences of the abyss? A few connections stand out above the rest. The most immediate thing we notice is that these experiences—at least as far as they have been recorded in his writings and those of others—give us no indication of a psychotic break. Beginning in 1600, with the confusion and melancholy brought on by his discovery of what he found to be such opposition in the world, "that in all things there was evil and good...and that it went as well in this world with the wicked as with the virtuous, honest, and Godly" (1915, pp. 485–87), Boehme's visions were noetic; they opened the gate to inner knowledge and gnosis, and produced a voluminous compendium of work. Also, Boehme exhibited a diminution rather than an inflation of ego as shown in the following, already-quoted passage from *The Way to Christ*: "If it were possible for him to remain quiet for an hour or less in his inner self-will and speaking, the divine will would speak into him" [*The Way to Christ*, p. 209].

Themes of opposition—of creation and destruction, good and evil, Christ and Lucifer, *Ungrund* and Sophia—abound in Boehme's map, themes that locate the original problem that so troubled him squarely—in light of Jung's insight—in the realm of the Self-field. Here, all naturally occurring oppositions of the psyche are encountered. They would be held in harmonic tension and united.

Let us explore for a moment one of these themes in Boehme's writings that reflects this. It is, in fact, the theme of primary opposition, the creation of the Divine Mirror, Sophia, without whom, Boehme says, God remains unconscious. Antoine Faivre has succinctly summarized Boehme's articulation of this "first event" in his book *Theosophy, Imagination, Tradition: Studies in Western Esotericism*:

> It is in issuing forth from this unutterable *Ungrund* that God conceives Himself as a subject, opposes Himself to Himself, engenders in Himself an infinity of ideas and of thoughts. A taking or seizing that is possible due to a mediating element —the first among all mediations—a mirror which no longer is exactly God, which is somehow outside Him, but which allows Him to know Himself in his multiplicity through the infinity of objects that already incarnate Him revealing His infinite fertility. This mirror, or this eye, is Sophia, Divine Wisdom. The *Objectum, the Gegenwurf*, in relation to God, she is also the ideal image of the world, of the universe, for she contains the ideal images of all individual

beings. The first theophany on the ontological plane, the first face of the One, which the One needs so as to be revealed in multiplicity, she is also the first manifestation of the infinite in the finite, of the Absolute in a thing which, in a certain manner, is already concrete. In the heart of divinity therefore exists a separating power (a *Schiedlichkeit*, a *Separator*), which is first manifested in the form of the Sophianic mirror. (Faivre, 2000, p. 138)

Sophia, for Boehme, is clearly not configured as anything analogous to the collective unconscious of Jung since she preexists. She is before being, before time. She does not cross over to the psychological realm. There are, nonetheless, some interesting parallels to the function of the Self and Self-field in Jung to Boehme's Sophia. Recalling Wickes's image of the Lonely One gazing into the Void and the Star that rises in response to the yearning of this One, Sophia is the "first event" of creation as well as the first opposition. God wills an "other" to reveal himself to himself. The forming of Sophia out of the abyss, according to Boehme, is God's first creative act. In *The Key*, Boehme also refers to Sophia as the "breathing of the Divine Power," who is a "Subject and Resemblance of the infinite and unsearchable Unity" (1991, p. 23).

> She is the true Divine Chaos, wherein all things lie, namely a Divine Imagination, in which the *Ideas* of Angels and Souls have been seen from eternity, in a Divine Type and resemblance; yet not then as Creatures, but in resemblance, as when a man beholds his face in a Glass: therefore the Angelical and human *Idea* flowed forth from the wisdom, and was formed into an Image. (Ibid.)

Reminiscent of the activity of the archetypal Self that involves a supraordinate ordering and unifying principle, Sophia's action is described by Faivre as "setting in motion in our universe the action of the essences" (Faivre, 2000, p. 139). As W. P. Swainson says, it is this "first event," this first opposition of God the Father (theo) and Wisdom (sophia), of these "two seemingly antagonistic, yet really complementary, forces or principles," that "underlies all manifestation" in creation. First, from the "Duality proceeds a Trinity," the joining of eternal father and mother "begets the Son, in Whom His-Her energies are concentrated or gathered up." Then comes "the generation of all things…the unmanifest becomes manifest, the latent becomes active" (Waite, 1940, pp. 93–95).

In *The Forty Questions of the Soul*, Boehme speaks further on the concept of the image and its relationship to the abyss, using a visual aid of an intricately drawn and meticulously labeled mandala of sorts,

> [T]he true image standeth in the abyss beyond all source, and dwelleth in nothing, *viz.*, in itself only, and through it God dwelleth, therefore there is nothing but the divine power that can find, move, or destroy it; for it is not in nature. (1911, pp. 52–53)

In an interesting convergence, not only does Jung reference Boehme's image of a "reversed eye" or "philosophical mirror" as an example of a mandala (1958, par. 136n), but Jung replicates and references the mandala of *Forty Questions* in *The Archetypes and the Collective Unconscious*, saying that Boehme "was the first to try to organize the Christian cosmos, as a total reality, into a mandala." He reports the failure of this attempt since, as he says, Boehme was "unable to unite the two halves in a circle." Jung tells us that rather than achieving such a union (i.e., completing the circle), in Boehme's depiction "the bright and dark semi-circles are turned back to back" (1959a, p. 341).

But was this what Boehme was attempting to do with this diagram? A careful reading of the words before, accompanying, and following the picture suggests that Boehme just might have had another goal in mind. Here are his own words with which he describes these circles, the very circles that Jung says are "back to back" (and, for the purposes of our discussion, descriptively, are reminiscent of spheres!):

> Those circles should be like round globes through which a cross should go, for it is the Eye of eternity, which cannot be portrayed; it representeth the Eye of the essence of all essences; the Eye of God, which is the glass of wisdom, wherein all wonders have been seen from eternity; and hereby is described how it is entered into an essence. (1911, p. 44)

Is it possible that Boehme was attempting to show in one diagram, not the entire Christian cosmos, but something else entirely? What is this "Eye of Eternity" that he speaks of? Does it connect with his pivotal vision of the eye in the pewter dish?

Further evidence of what he means can be found in "A Short Summary Appendix of the Soul," which appears at the end of *The Forty Questions of the Soul*. In it, Boehme writes,

> *The soul is an eye in the eternal abyss, a similitude of eternity* [italics mine], a perfect figure and image of the first Principle, and resembleth God the Father in

his Person, as to the eternal nature....And so the soul also appeared out of the eternal center of nature, out of the eternal essence. (Ibid., pp. 202–3)

Could this "eye in the eternal abyss" be the same as the "Eye of Eternity?" Is "the Eye of the essence of all essences" the same as what "appeared out of the eternal center of nature, out of the eternal essence?" Sometimes, Boehme's seventeenth-century prose can be dense and confusing. In this case, however, the answer would appear to be clearly "yes" on both counts. It would seem, then, from these two passages that Boehme was not attempting to diagram the entire Christian cosmos. It appears that he was trying, rather, to map the soul.

Let us see what Boehme means by soul as we examine further his writings and his diagram. First, he compares the receptive quality of the soul to the moon receiving light from the sun. Both receive and reflect back the source of the light. As I have described earlier, a manifestation of reception pertains to the soul opening like a female womb receiving and giving of seed by the same token.

In his diagram, Boehme places the soul in the abyss ("an eye in the eternal abyss"), as he does Sophia. He speaks of the one in language similar to what he uses to describe the other. He says the soul "resembleth God the Father in his person." Of Sophia, Faivre recites Boehme's concept of "a mirror...which allows Him to know Himself." Both act as mirrors, but the one (the soul) is subsidiary to the other (Sophia). Faivre goes on to elucidate that it is Sophia who,

translates the divine Word into forms and colors, that are already semi-real, that is, distinct from God who, by means of them, knows Himself as a person and will in His turn be knowable. One thinks of this beautiful verse from Koranic esotericism, which has the Lord say: "I was a hidden treasure, I aspired to be known." (Faivre, 2000, p. 138)

Thus, "Sophia is the eye, the mirror, that the *Ungrund* imagines in order to introduce itself into it, to take form so to speak by means of the images that this living mirror will send back to it" (Faivre, 2000, p. 160). And we are the receiving mirror (in this image) of a double pregnancy. The soul directs itself in imagination into the Father (*Ungrund*, unknown) to be fertilized by Him (spirit) in turn. In this image, the "eye" reflects an eye in a pewter dish and mirroring becomes secondary, in a sense, to the reality of the event itself. It is impossible to tell who is mirroring whom (von Franz, 1975, p. 38). As this exchange occurs between spirit and the womb of the human soul, divinity is re-engendered and always new. We reenact in human form the process of exchange between the divine, original parents. This exchange effects a unity of soul and matter in that soul receives spirit, and spirit takes matter into itself as matter is reflected back and in, and through, the living mirror.

This is what I am saying underlies the experience of unitary reality of Jung and Boehme and others. We are remembering the original unity, the original pre-differentiated nature that was of the undifferentiated abyss/void/ Pleroma, and that is what Boehme and Jung are pointing to. They "see straight through to a specific reality." For Boehme, the ground of the Trinity is the *Ungrund* (in symbol/visionary form). We live in the image of the image of the preexistent eternal and this fact needs to be remembered, which means spirit *in* the body, deep feeling, experience.

In depth psychology, we also "remember" through the soul. Ulanov makes the point, drawing from Jung (1921, par. 424), that the soul,

> "is a function of relation between the subject and the inaccessible depths of the unconscious. The determining force (God) operating from these depths is reflected by the soul, that is, it creates symbols and images." The soul is then "both receiver and transmitter," perceives unconscious contents and conveys them to consciousness by means of these symbols." The soul lives, as it were, midway between the ego and the primordial unconscious, which expresses itself through the archetypal images that the soul receives, creates, and transmits. (Ulanov, 1999b, p. 21)
>
> The soul is thus like a two-way mirror, reflecting unconscious to ego and ego to unconscious. (Ibid., p. 31)

In essence, I am saying that to live in the image of the image there is something we need to make conscious that is unconscious and unintegrated. This state of unintegration is part of our being human.

How many mirrors does it take to receive and engender the ever new? All it takes is one person, one artist, one mystic, one floor trader, one mother, one CEO, one professor, one editor, one human being. Jung tells us that "maybe one would do." It takes only one to suffer into being what feels like no being at all, the death, a symbolic death that Jung tells us accompanies a conscious reconciliation of the opposites. Jung says that this conscious *coniunctio* has the effect of continuously incarnating the God image (1975, p. 510ff).

The symbolic death that Jung speaks of is like being on a cross gazing into the void, or staring into the empty tomb. It feels very lonely. It may feel like a blackhole void of antimatter since what one is confronting is what is truly *un-conscious*. It is totally other than anything the ego knows. The experience is one of spirit trying to come into matter. This coming into being is the reason for being created and the gift we have as humans: to recognize the true underlying reality of what we can see through to in unitary reality. This is no ordinary mysticism.

These two men brought into consciousness an awareness of the chthonic spirit, spirit in matter. In Boehme's case, newly formed consciousness informed a collective situation in which post-Reformation Christianity increasingly separated spirit from matter. For Jung, conscious awareness of the Self connects the ego to the unconscious and offers a window to eternity. Jung's notion of the archetypal Self is analogous to Boehme's mirrored reflection of Sophia, Wisdom. Sophia, the heavenly Mother who does not cross over into the material world but who remains preexistent in eternal conjunction, eternally reflective of the original ground. Soul, for Boehme then, is the reflected presence of Sophia; a reflection of the image of the Trinity, the activity of spirit coming into matter, working through the Self of the unconscious—in Jung's terms—so that it can incarnate through us.

Lessons for Clinical Practice:
Depth Psychology and the
Radical Other of Soul

The experience of the abyss/Pleroma is particularly germane and helpful to the clinical setting. Jung and Boehme both bring back from the experience and develop over time their own map for understanding the radical otherness of this preexistent unitary reality. Jung's experience of unitary reality underscores how psychology needs the transcendent realm of spirit to engage in a truly depth-psychological process.

The fact of unitary reality leads Jung to spend his life describing his map, the nature and contents of the collective unconscious as the container of ultimacy and depth for the clinical procedure of analytical psychology. The collective unconscious is, for Jung, the medium through which we apprehend and keep alive a grasp of what exists at the layer of the abyss, of spirit. For Jung, the presence of the transcendent as spirit is experienced by the psyche in the form of an archetype, a psychic center linked to instinct and characterized by the features of numinosity, autonomy, and unconsciousness. An archetype is expressed by a symbol that is a captivating, although enigmatic, portrayal of psychic reality often leading us toward a conscious position contrary to our current one. Attending to symbolic process means that the ego must relate to the unconscious contents of the psyche: dreams, waking fantasies, or behavior, contrary to or other than whatever position the ego holds.

As we correspond with this presence via an exercise of reflection, a third factor or position emerges through what

Jung calls the transcendent function. A symbol begins to unfold in pictorial, tactile, or auditory statements and images that indicate a synthesis of the opposing elements and a resolution to the conscious conflict (Jung, 1921, par. 825). Attending to this conscious-unconscious process is analogous to living a symbolic life in which we come partially to understand the specific meaning of our individual symbols that, simultaneously, point toward, and participate in, their archetypal source. Boehme calls this third, Christ—the product of Theo and Sophia; Jung calls it the Self or the center. Christ is preexistent in that he is of the same essence as the original ground. The Self, according to von Franz,

> extends far beyond the dimensions of the individual ego, and in truth, we find in observing the unconscious and its manifestations that it possesses dimensions that are impossible to delimit. (1994, p. 329)

Where psychology often can be most deficient, ironically, is in its lack of insight into the dynamics of soul. If, however, psychology purports to probe the *depth* of the human psyche, does not such a psychology of *depth* have the special task of attempting to understand soul? Among depth psychologists who at least address the activity of soul, Jung stands out.

Jung defines soul as the heart or essence of the person endowed with the potential for a conscious relationship to Deity (1968, par. 9, 10, 11). He derives his clinical facts from the departure point of lived experience of what transcends us, what is numinous. For Jung, we each have a religious function and instinct. Our relation to the religious function of the psyche provides a reference point outside the collective mass for the archetypal influences that can sweep us away.

Attentiveness to this innate capacity, called *soul*, gives us the strength to deal with paradox that we usually reject and/or rationalize out of experience. The symbols of soul that arise from primordial experience can bind us to the treasury of shared experience in our particular religious tradition. Look to symbols, Jung says (Jung, 1956, pars. 114, 344), and track the themes that recur in symbolic form, for they combine the opposites of our personal conflicts, and/or shared human conflicts, such as dark and light, creation and destruction, eros and aggression, death and life, which exist in all of us. The conscious embracing of opposites can lead us toward the fullness and richness of human experience.

Analyst and patient often find themselves at an interesting crossroads where they can either bind or disconnect through the dynamics of soul. Does the analyst turn away from this juncture? Hopefully not.

We become plump with questions: What does it mean for the soul to be in an ongoing, open dialogue with the psyche as defined by depth psychology? The objective psyche, as Jung describes it, is a bridge to what truly exists beyond the psyche, before being as we typically conceptualize it. We need the psyche to apprehend the fact of transcendent ultimacy.

Boehme's understanding of Sophia as Divine Mirror is helpful because he introduces us, in the language of Christianity, to the concept of the opposites on all levels of being. In Boehme's view of things, opposition is a good and necessary condition to self-knowledge and love. When God desired to know himself, he created Sophia. The first divine event was also the first opposition. From opposition of otherness in the psyche is born the third.

This is familiar language to depth psychology. Jung recognized this as a function of the psyche, the transcendent function. Self-knowledge is required on the path toward individuation, which is a process of making the unconscious into the conscious, the "hidden treasure" into the "known."

Without the soul, as Jung defines it, and the conditions facilitating experience of the soul as passionately compelling the total personality, we miss the flesh of a truly symbolic life in which symbols arise in immediate religious and psychological experience.

In primary process—what Jung experienced in his own years of breakdown and breakthrough and that he came to call *nondirected thinking*—we find ourselves engaged with the subjective language of affect, instinct, and image, as well as the objective process of the unconscious. Jung contrasts nondirected thinking with what he calls directed thinking. In directed thinking (what Freud called primary process), our conscious rationality dominates (Jung, 1956, pp. 16, 29).

Jung's emphasis upon nondirected thinking is particularly susceptible to the dilemmas of objectification and depersonalization that we encounter as clinicians in our postmodern era. As a result of the cultural predominance of directed thinking, the transformation of our reality into images on the plane of projection often dominates. We end up rejecting claims of universal truth with the assertion that there can be no unifying knowledge. We find unincarnated mush in contrast to enfleshed soul and symbol as we are assaulted mercilessly by the postmodern, pop-cultural, pop-psych, superficial, disconnected, and ungrounded likes of Po-Mo cyborg chic and *Tripmaster Monkey*.

Wheras Oprah and Jerry Springer may offer inexplicably epiphanal experiences for some in the space of television illusion, we need also to look to where our projective identifications lead. Part of the difficulty with projective identification is that it becomes reification (investing popular idols, things, and objects with reality) in that we *are* trying to project ourselves into something larger in order to experience what is Wholly Other, what is unifying; but we somehow miss the prospective, forward-moving and symbolic value of the ways in which we projectively identify. In part, this is due to what I explain in the following chapter as fear and/or resistance to emotions and images of depth. We end up merged in identification with objects or, at the other extreme, bored, with our libido withdrawn and cathected pregenitally when we could be otherwise pursuing with fuller ego consciousness our nondirected thinking and our libidinal desire at more archaic levels in which we might eventually incorporate symbols and let go of what is more narrowly objectified.

If we choose to affirm and receive radical otherness, then the soul, as Jung defines it, becomes the province of depth psychology, and we find ourselves engaged in a willing receptivity toward the symbols that give us a sense of both the soul's presence and its archetypal source. The question becomes one of "how do we receive a Self so large and maintain personal identity in relation to the dynamic transcendent in a way in which we can bring something of what we find back into life?"

Unitary reality, as I am defining it and as I believe Jung to have encountered it through his experiences of the unconscious, bridges to a certain reality where we temporarily lose what we know to the unknown and come back to our conscious reality replete with a fullness of imagery, even though we may not quite be able to explain the experience itself. There is something about the nature of unitary reality that I believe Jung and Boehme came to know in the *Ungrund*/Pleroma experience that is so radically other that it brings something completely new into existence, perhaps even restructuring the entire personality in a way the ego can better deal with its context and circumstances.

In the clinical example that follows, I would like to address the presence of the soul and its archetypal source with the purpose of exploring clinical practice in the context of unitary reality. The Pleroma and *Ungrund*, as expressions of the abyss, are important in terms of a specific kind of experience in the clinical setting and are related to what becomes known in and through the collective unconscious.

First, I will give concrete illustrations from a six-year treatment (with permission to do so from the individual illustrated), then underscore what, in the meeting of psychoanalysis and spirit, I feel Jung and Boehme give us in terms of acknowledgment of unitary reality that makes a difference in sustaining clinical depth.

7

MEETING CLINICAL OTHERNESS

WHAT DOES THE knowledge that Boehme and Jung bring back from the abyss tell us that is helpful and meaningful clinically? How is unitary reality experienced in the room between analyst and patient? What is the nature of the knowledge that the ego brings back from the experience and the kind of change that can take place? How does this "all and nothing" and "everything in potential," images of which Boehme and Jung have given us, appear in the patient's dreams and images? What does the therapist witness as a change in emotional tone as the patient meets this reality? What is the experience of the abyss like as the ego lets go of defenses and sinks into the unknown, losing control of what the person believes to have been his or her primary ground? What distinguishes the layer of radical otherness in contrast to the layers of projection or the primordial?

We can begin to address some of these questions by underscoring the notion that the experience of unitary reality and knowledge of it makes a difference in clinical work. The fact of this inherent psychological reality contains and makes room for all forms of otherness to be experienced and integrated.

The familiar slogan from television favorites like Star Trek, "space—the final frontier," seems limited when I think of the concept of "finality." When I think of the vastness of the territory of the unconscious yet unexplored, I am reminded of the notion of "many mansions," a New Testament scriptural image analogous to the psyche, which is so expansive that we have only begun to fathom it.

Such a worldview is completely the opposite of a metaphysical or epistemological box or a hermetically closed system. Quite in contrast to a Cartesian-Kantian paradigm, "in which experience of the unitive numinous depths of reality has been systematically extinguished" (Tarnas, 1991, p. 12), the collective unconscious points to direct knowledge of reality beyond the archetypes themselves. And yet, at the same time, the nature of the collective unconscious gives us a priori archetypal forms at a more personal, developmental, cultural level.

But even the personal, archetypal forms point. They lead beyond being merely the deepest patterns of human projection, or inherited structures that precede human experience. Jung came closest to this conception of the archetypes in his study of synchronicity as he began to understand that unitary reality implies autonomous patterns of meaning that inhere in both psyche and matter.

Bearing the above in mind, in therapy, we begin where the patient is. Anything that is other in terms of a person's conscious image of self or an image of self that does not exist yet in a person's frame of experience (because it is unconscious), potentially can become the pregnant reality that is held "eye-to-eye" between the two persons in the therapeutic setting. "Pleromatic" experience gets us in touch particularly with what is "not yet." Something arises in the therapeutic from the abyss of unknowing, from unconscious to consciousness.

Through our experience of the unconscious, we bridge to a certain reality where we temporarily lose what we know to the unknown and come back to our conscious reality replete with at least a small fishnet of new or unexplored imagery, even though we may not quite be able to explain the experience itself. If this sounds like mysticism, it is not in the sense that it is an esoteric experience available only to contemplatives. In the therapeutic setting, there will be moments when one or both persons in the room feel that their ego-selves are surrendered to something quite unknown that many would identify as "something divine," or something extraordinarily "other."

In my work with one particular patient, I found myself, in the early years of our work, entering mutually into a temporary trance state on a rather regular basis. At a certain point in the session, words would just stop, and we would sit in silence as if held together in a magnetic field. The patient's face would flush and there was a strong feeling of eros and aliveness, although not sexualized.

I chose not to break into the mesmerism of these trances until he came out of them spontaneously. I could tell that these were a place of the unknown, a place where the memory, desire, and will of the ego gets suspended and relinquished to what "is not yet."

In the early years of our work, images did not arise for him—just this very strong affect—the affect of being united, unitary, one. He could hardly find words for this experience because he was *in* it and his ego was temporarily pushed aside. The oneness was not created by either of us. It was as if a giant magnet stopped our thoughts from flowing, powerfully so, and drew up all the psychic energy into one center. I, too, felt my ego-self fall away.

We'd sit in this patient's place of "I don't know" for as long as it took. Countertransferentially, I felt awkward at first, as if I were allowing the patient to indulge in something too vulnerable or intrapsychically incestuous. Initially, these "intervals" lasted for what felt like long periods of time.

Yet, these trancelike states took us right into the core of his transference to strong, dominating women like his mother. He had a radiant glow to his skin and a slightly impish gleam in his eyes as if, momentarily, there were no hierarchy in the room (transferentially so) in which a maternal figure held the authority over him. This submission was the one pole. The other was his well-defended, insulated personality that kept him at quite a distance in terms of his deep feelings (anger, sadness, longing).

In time, allowing both these poles to exist in the room in the transference, images began to pour forth as his muse developed internally, as a positive (although rather nubile) anima. He composed lyrics to songs, took his work to a studio, and finally, years later, has produced two CDs that tell the story of his inner life. The first was entitled "Crossing Streams."

The more elementary and negative Great mother still hovers and penetrates our sessions cyclically, but he is more able to temper these energies than be overcome by them (i.e., getting into rageful fights with his wife, coming late to sessions, threatening to stop his therapy because his wife said it wasn't fixing him—to her satisfaction).

The above is just a very brief vignette to demonstrate how, in the clinical setting, we definitely recognize when something completely new comes into existence, something that can even restructure the entire personality of the patient in a way that the ego can deal creatively with its context and circumstances.

More often, however, at least in my experience, unitary reality is the culmination of a long process of encounter in which struggle and suffering are present, and both patient and analyst meet all forms of otherness.

PAULA

I was told that "the other little girl" was killed and buried in the basement under the place where the water ran through from the washing machine. I was told I'd be killed, too. Every time I heard the water run through, I'd get terrified. I also was told I'd be locked in the barn in the room where the rabbits were killed and the rats and the raccoons would get me and kill me, too.

I woke up at 3:30 A.M. with this image before me. I see this bird lying on the ground and, while looking at this bird, the character from the *Bad Seed*, a very evil child who kills and harms other children, is saying: "Don't worry. It's not dead; it's just sleeping. It's only stunned."

I'm thinking about how I always cried when I was between four and six, and whenever my mom asks me what I'm crying about, I say "I don't know."

I still remember my mom saying, "Remember the special prayers," and I do. I pray for God to bring things hidden in the darkness into the light (with permission from patient Paula, whose name I have changed to protect her anonymity, personal communication, 2001).

A young married woman of thirty, comes into treatment fearing that she will certainly die if she gives birth. She has grown up as the eighth of fifteen siblings in a Roman Catholic family, and had to become a mother to her mother who died of cancer, as well as to the seven younger siblings who remain at home. Her father turns to alcohol to deal with his grief and comes home from work demanding dinner on the table. A few years later, he is hit by a car, killed, trying to protect a new female partner from being hit by the speeding vehicle on the highway.

The young woman's dreams portray apocalyptic events, an impending end that obliterates everything in life, including herself. A few months into our work, she becomes pregnant by her husband. She dreams that all mothers and children will be indiscriminately slaughtered in a country at war reminiscent of Bosnia. God does not intervene. God is a dominantly male God of ideals and judgment. She cannot reach an accepting God, through prayers to her mother, through me, or through her church community. Having converted away from Catholicism, she cannot find a church home where she feels comfortable and safe.

Psychological breakdown impends. She makes it almost through the term of pregnancy and then leaves treatment with me one month before delivering. Three months later, I am rushed away to the West Coast to deal with my own mother's sudden death. This patient calls for me during my absence. She has given birth to a baby girl with her husband

and has had repetitive waking dreams of an impending apocalyptic event, which she refers to as her visions. The unconscious material is much closer to the surface and, this time, has effected a breakdown, an interlude where she is overwhelmed by psychic contents and besieged by fears that she and her newborn child, a little girl, will die.

When I return from family responsibilities, we resume treatment. In her first renewed session with me, she admits her hesitation around recommitting to treatment, feeling out whether or not I will be able to hold her breakdown having just lost my own mother. She is reassured.

The months go by, and as her little girl begins to walk she asks if she can bring her along to our sessions since she cannot find a babysitter whom she trusts. I agree to this because I feel something is being worked out at a deeper level. At this point, she also changes from one Protestant church to another, and becomes somewhat comfortable with a female minister.

In our work, the consulting room begins to take on an entirely new tonality as a ritual forms around the arrival and departure of the stroller now bearing her ten-month-old child. She changes the child's diaper, goes to the restroom with me watching the child for a few minutes, then unpacks the child's toys and a snack. Fisher-Price dolls are strewn across the floor. Raisin bits, pretzel crumbs, and carrot nubs are crushed into the carpet. My Kleenex box goes empty while the child delights in pretending to blow her nose.

All the while, the mother and I never lose sight of each other, even though there is nonstop jabber going on as the little child talks to imaginary people on my telephone, plays peek-a-boo behind my chair, and gets stuck under a table with her Barney. The young mother and I remain connected even in the distraction.

Then, slowly, another ritual ensues. The young woman, Paula, begins to elucidate selected passages to me from her journal on a regular basis, recounting painful childhood events and traumas. She does not read from it, but lifts it out of her satchel, thumbs through highlighted sections, and speaks of particular images. Soon, she begins to dream again.

After another three or four months go by, she is able to both pray for her mother and to be angry with her at the same time. In her prayer life, she begins also to forgive her mother for neglecting her in the chaos of fourteen other children, "My mother had another child every time she was overwhelmed," Paula said. "I was devastated that she never sewed me a rag doll like she did for all my sisters."

That week, Paula dreams that her mother comes down to her and sits with her on a sofa where Paula is smoking a cigar. Her mother shows her how to clip off the end and tells her about a great coffee to go with the cigar. In reality, the mother had smoked a great deal and had died of lung cancer. Paula admitted to having smoked cigars along with drinking a brandy while on vacation with her husband. "Maybe I'm becoming someone that I don't know I am?" she said.

Tremendous fears prevail. Apocalyptic themes arise again from her unconscious around the event of the Bush-Gore election. Similar to her certainty that the world would end with the coming of the millennium, she asks "Will I always be so paranoid?" but adds, "I have been thinking that Kathryn might be able to really help me [using my name even though I was right there]. I've been thinking that I never have had the experience of *knowing* that I was loved." She added a budding insight: "I wonder if some of my religious beliefs and fears, and things that hold me back, are not based more upon suspicion than on faith."

Her dream of a cigar-smoking mother presented a surprising image for her. It spoke of a strange otherness emerging in her psyche.

She dreams again. She is an adult walking into a room where there is a large mirror. In the mirror, she sees reflected the image of her mother holding a tiny infant, patting its little body. The mother is headless. Next to her mother in the mirror is a small girl almost out of the mirror, reaching up toward Paula as the adult dream ego enters the room.

This dream proves too arresting for her to talk about immediately. We go at it gently. She stops bringing her own little girl to sessions because I delicately suggest that it seems she wants me to be very present to what is going on inside her. I never addressed her bringing the child as a resistance. The ritual of the child had its own momentum and to do anything else would have foreclosed on the unfolding of images in her psyche. We were a threesome: the archetypal Great Mother (in its negative form as destructive, annihilating, empty; in its positive form in her transference to me), Paula, and her little girl (cf. Jung, 1959a, par. 148 ff.).

Further, I was a positive figure for Paula in that I mothered Paula's mothering. Meanwhile, a symbol was forming, but not one that she would have expected.

Weeks later, in the context of the headless-mother dream, she announced with deep and sad feeling: "The core is this nothingness. This *space* of nothing." Identified with the "bad" attributed to her by her family (seventeen in all, including the parents), the void was great. The apocalyptic feelings of death and obliteration began to make some sense for her as connected not only to her mother's death and her actual witnessing of it, not only to the actual abuse and neglect of other family members in relation to her, but also to a memory of a death of a different kind.

As Neumann says,

> The child develops from a stage of life antecedent to the ego, from a pre-personal existence in a cosmic world where the personal mother *is* the child (Neumann, 1989 p. 84). The mother of the primal relationship guarantees a cosmos—a world ordered in her own image. The existence of the child—its life or death—is dependent on the nourishing, protecting, warmth, giving, ordering, and balancing power of the mother (Ibid., p. 80). The growing child is enclosed within the mother's psyche as part of its unconscious and conscious existence (Ibid., p. 82). The child does not distinguish between its own body and its mother's body. (Ibid., p. 80)

For Paula, this "cosmos," this "body," had been severed developmentally at some level of early trauma, as was evident in the headless mother of her dream. Her potentialities in terms of unitary reality, or a felt oneness, could not "fulfill themselves in an empty space" (Ibid., p. 82).

On the other hand, both hope and dread were visible in the split of the mirror. On the left side of the mirror was a headless mother, analogous to an abyss of emptiness, an emptiness that feels like death to an infant who experiences no reflection of itself and has no somatic memory of a "bodily cosmos." On the right side of the mirror was a little girl, reaching out for love and *knowing* that she might become known, re-membered. The little girl sees herself reflected in the dream ego, and the dream ego sees its own reflection in the little girl's reaching out. This "exchange" between the dream figures paralleled what was happening in the room between Paula, the little girl, and me.

This patient, whose religious faith leaned toward the charismatic, wanted so passionately to believe in an inflated way that her visions were of prophetic import. She went from pastor to pastor relating her story for affirmation of being a prophet of forthcoming events.

I could have whittled down her visions into the dust of paranoid delusion, which would have left her in a deflation. I could have interpreted her resistance when the presence of her child bordered on distracting both of us from the center of our work; but the child seemed to be the link to Paula's missing experience, an absence that had to be first experienced as a series of abysses, accompanied by great suffering.

There was the bodily abyss. Paula was becoming more and more conscious, painfully so, of her own inability to be at home in the bodily space of mothering. To play with her child frustrated her and induced in her feelings of depression in relation to her perceived inadequacy. At the extreme, she feared what she might do to the child if left too long alone with it in the room with the anguish she experienced as a mother. She also admitted to deep feelings of shame and discomfort in relation to her body image weight-wise and, more critically, to her tremendous fear and sensitivity around having sexual relations with her husband especially in the context of his wanting to have another child.

There was the abyss of "mother and mothering" in terms of the great loss and limitation of her own overburdened mother and the amplification of this gap of mothering in relation to me. She wanted something from me but struggled to relinquish herself to become more dependent upon me. For instance, when she would become truly unable to cope with day-to-day affairs, she would call her physician (a female), and ask for an antidepressant and not tell me about it for weeks: thus, leaving me out of her depth of feeling. At the same time, it became increasingly difficult for her to leave our sessions without great sadness and tears that would take us beyond our time.

Another level of abyss, and the most transformative one, was the abyss of the little girl, the one who did not yet exist consciously. Through her child's relationship to me, my comfort in playing with her child, and the trust between the child and me, Paula was confronted with the fact of her own internals. She did not have available to consciousness the memory of play in relation to her own mother. Something new existed alongside this absence: the spirit-in-the-body "cosmos" of play and playing. Paula had to experience the abyss at all these levels in order for the nothing to become a something in which Paula could experience a presence. What exactly is this presence?

In even such a brief case example, many questions arise: How does the transcendent function? Is the transcendent functioning in the patient's desire and longing, in her beginning to realize how much she wanted me to love her? Is the transcendent functioning in our mutual adoration of the patient's child whereby my love for the child gets mirrored back to the patient and is increasingly present in the images of self in her dreams? Do we encounter the transcendent only as a function in the psyche? What are we considering to be transcendent? Is the functioning of the transcendent something other than the two people in the room? How do we distinguish the otherness of the analytic relationship from other levels of being, primordial, or radical otherness that may be present?

Is there such a thing as an absolute moment of encounter with the transcendent? If so, what is the content of this moment? Is it present in the moment Paula has the dream? Is it her remembering the dream and her relating the dream imagery to me? Is the moment that of her own insight when she amplifies the dream? Is it Paula's conscious realization of the nothingness at the core, the absence of presence in her own transitional space (cf. for instance, Winnicott, 1962)? Is the absolute moment the nothingness itself? Or the love itself? Or both? What is transcendent? Is everything unconscious transcendence?

I would begin to address these questions by saying that the transcendent has something to do with the inbreaking of radical otherness in contradistinction to the layers of projection/introjection and the primordial (or, in this case, the personal unconscious), although all these layers contribute toward our getting a glimpse of the unitary reality, or oneness, that underlies all psychological experience.

With Paula, for instance, the layer of spirit has to do with the space of nothingness that also holds potential and fullness, the dread *and* hope in unity. When the ego can house the original memory of breakdown (the traumatic loss of original unity, for example), the new can break through. We see this represented in the flesh of the moment that the dream ego sees its potentiality in the mirrored reality of the little girl and at the moment this potentiality becomes a consciously lived reality in the physical flesh of the body of the analytic relationship.

Recalling the earlier analogy of mirror, I am speculating that the experience of soul occurs somewhere between the center of the sphere (the psychoid unconscious) and the principal focus (the ego), the center of the sphere being analogous to the Self-ego axis. The image of the little girl is a compensatory image, the inverse, a potential for aliveness and the new who appears initially as a mirrored reality (literally in this dream), in other words, not yet consciously related to.

PAUL RICŒUR AND THE ROLE OF THE SYMBOLIC

In short, otherness can be considered in terms of projective and introjective otherness: the *me* and *not me* of the psyche. We do this all the time by making subject and object distinctions about specific groups or individuals in culture. We objectify and/or depersonalize them, or miss soul-to-soul connectedness altogether.

Have you noticed that people truly seem to have lost their ability to listen to each other? The "dark side" of the totally connected world we live in today is that we seem to feel more isolated from one another. (Which is why, I suppose, the profession of psychotherapy is on the rise.) We're so glutted with "messages" coming to us from every quarter 24/7/365. In addition to all the voicemail, e-mail, spam, instant messages, and text messages; ads pop up in our faces on computer screens at home, at work, at the

ATM, in the back of taxicabs. All channels of communication seem to be full, yet are any of them really working very well?

Another factor of disconnection and depersonalization is that of meaninglessness. In the spring of 1932, when the practice of psychoanalysis was still relatively new, Carl Jung observed at a conference in Strasbourg that, "Among all my patients in the second half of life—that is to say, over thirty-five—there has not been one whose problems in the last resort was not that of finding a religious outlook in life" (CW 11, par. 488–538).

Jung recognized that many deep psychological problems of the adult in treatment—including depression, anxiety, relational difficulties, sleeplessness—were essentially problems of meaning and that addressing problems of meaning was the natural realm of religion.

On a more philosophical and spiritual level, Paul Ricœur speaks of this problem of meaning as resulting in our worship of the "religious object" in contrast to the "Wholly Other." He speaks of the wholly other and the religious object in the context of immanence and transcendence with the implication that the Wholly Other may, in truth, be beyond all of our categories of understanding. Yet, he believes that the Wholly Other draws near to us whereas the religious object does not.

In *Freud and Philosophy: An Essay on Interpretation*, Ricœur emphasizes the radical otherness of the transcendent, which we experience through the role of the symbolic. At the same time, he warns us that there are two rather perilous directions we can take that are inherent to a philosophy of immanence.

The first wrong turn we can make is that, once we begin to sense the profound experience of the Wholly Other, we empty ourselves into the transcendent. In so doing, we actually eliminate the fact of otherness.

Ricœur describes this action as operating at the level of secondary and derived forms of illusion (i.e., projection), which leads to the death of the religious object. Thinking collectively, Ricœur emphasizes that otherness is a necessary factor in the evolution and culmination of human history. Otherness, at the level of the Wholly Other gives human history its prophetical and eschatological import (Ricœur, 1970, p. 529).

A second hazardous viewpoint, Ricœur tells us, derives from our attempt to objectify the Wholly Other and use it to fill our emptiness. For example, we transform the sacred into a new sphere of objects, institutions, and powers. Although this kind of objectification is a step up from secondary, derived forms of illusion, it is still an attempt to transform transcendent spirit into an object. This object may feel sacred to us, in other words, more than a mere sign, but spiritually speaking, faith at this level still derives from "that region of the symbolic where the horizon-function is constantly being reduced to the object-function" (Ibid., p. 530). To unpack "horizon-function," and "object-function" in psychological terms, this would mean that the transcendent (beyond psyche) becomes yet another cultural or religious object at the first or second level of otherness I have spoken of, rather than the ego-Self sphere.

The ego-Self sphere pertains to the formation in the individual of a unitary world accompanied by a centered experience of unity (Neumann, 1989 p. 57). Jung wrote of the relationship between the ego and the Self as two great psychic streams that need each other. Without the ego, the Self remains without a presence in the everyday world (Jung, 1958, par. 391, passim). Another way of speaking about the ego-Self relationship was coined by Edinger as the "ego-Self axis."

> The ego-Self axis represents the vital connection between the ego and Self that must be relatively intact if the ego is to survive stress and grow. The axis is the gateway or path of communication between the conscious personality and the archetypal psyche. Damage to the ego-Self axis impairs or destroys the connection between conscious and unconscious, leading to alienation of the ego from its origin and foundation. (Edinger, 1972, p. 38)

As in the spherical mirror, the ego-Self axis would be analogous to a "passing through," in which the ego would be the intersecting plane for the Self and the Self for the ego. This would mean that, potentially, the ego would share in the attributes of the Self-sphere. In aligning with the Self, it is aligning with the axis that runs through the "center" of the psyche, the psychoid, archetypal layer. The sharing of attributes recalls Jung's notion of psyche and matter being but a mirror in some way of each other.

The Self as the middle point of the mirror also intersects the other end of the spectrum, or *speculum*. A sphere has center *and* circumference. Then the ego-Self alliance would partake of both center and circumference. And because "circumference" does not necessarily imply an end point or a closed system in Jung's psychology, the Self may bridge to the beyond psyche, or what created psyche.

Thus, here we tread upon boundary-less-ness of the unknown in which the ego opens itself to continuous interpenetration, seduction, and allure by something quite other and beyond its own circumference so that the incarnation of transcendence can occur. Potentially being binds with being.

In the process of ego-Self alignment, images from this frontier of the unknown arise in the psyche, images that the ego has not created, images that need to be bound together in the body and in relationship, and in culture. We might call these images of spirit. What do we do with these images of spirit in the process of binding? Do we interpret them? Worship them? Ignore them? How are images of psyche and soul different from symbols of the sacred?

We are essentially wrestling with the question: Is surface depth? In other words, is what we see always (and only) what we get? Or does authentic depth point to a transcendent ultimacy beyond it that continuously encroaches upon, seduces, dismembers, and transforms surface immediacy? If there is this intentional transformative movement toward wholeness, then how do we maintain the openness and sturdiness it takes to sustain this archetypal imperative?

We are cast into the pit of psychological dismemberment, separation, differentiation from one to two, to a possible three-ness and, as Jung tells us, potentially at the level of the *mysterium coniunctionus*, a four-ness—all this emerging from an original oneness, to a return, a resurrection that entails once again a unitary reality, but from an entirely different point of view from which we began.

Knowing what is entailed, it is easy for us to lose the tension of this otherness in the face of the unknown, the "nothingness" before us. It is almost easier and less painful for us to succumb to ambiguity and watch while the symbols of our patients (and ourselves, and those of our culture) disintegrate into idols.

Yet, when depth psychology confuses surface for depth, the tension of contradiction needed to embrace the transcendent can get flattened out, in which case the encounter with the transcendent as radical otherness remains out of reach. Yet, ironically, the immediacy of our experience is crucial, as it provides the essential container and ground for the incarnation of transcendence.

The essential point is that, if we remain mired solely in a philosophy of immanence, we can fall into a hermeneutic of demystification, a deconstructive or constructive method of interpretation that drains the life out of the symbol.

A solely immanent point of view reduces the symbols of the sacred to mere cultural factors in a kind of admixture with our personal images. In other words, if we amplify our personal images only horizontally (immanently from Ricœur's view), without a transcendent other, we fuel breadth, but miss depth. The end result can present itself as multicultural*ism*, a disembodied ideology, in contrast to an embodied and relational cultural interdependence.

Philosophy of Transcendence

At the other extreme of a purely immanent view, there is the danger of a philosophy of *transcendence*, which eliminates the psyche altogether. Clinically speaking, this would translate as a therapist feeling his or her job is to enable the patient to be taken up into the higher category of salvation. Clearly, this therapist would be proceeding from a countertransference in which the therapist is confusing himself or herself as an instrument of divine grace. Since the therapist, too, is a seeker and one who must be wary of the inflation of having the ability "to cure" the patient, we must constantly examine our own *need* to heal another.

> The willingness to participate in such freedom [as grace] means that God *will* do the work. If freedom is uncertainty, then what is "normative" for us, including our deeply embraced theological convictions, must also be submitted to grace. (Madden, 1996, p. 363)

If a countertransference "to cure or to save" is the primary motivation of the therapist, both sign and symbol are in danger of being eradicated at the level of individual experience. We end up with another imbalance, a transcendent otherness that the patient struggles to reach. With such impingement on the part of the therapist, in terms of having an end goal, the patient can miss the value of human experience, the real stuff of the trenches. The patient can remain contentedly merged with the therapist's ideals. The therapist can miss the genuine otherness of the patient, the two-ness necessary for the transcendent function to come alive. At worst, both therapist and patient may feel stranded somewhere on the brink of a great ontological divide, stripped of the flesh of the psyche as a way to seek and connect with the transcendent (Ibid., p. 364).

The challenge for a therapist with any kind of religious, spiritual, or faith convictions, including atheism and agnosticism, is to maintain the integrity of the psyche while being conscious of the dangers of proclamation, which often emerge from unresolved countertransference needs.

Countertransference refers to feelings and images that are induced in the analyst by the patient. For instance, the therapist may feel helpless, or feel that the patient is helpless and needs rescue or special knowledge and insight from the therapist. An analyst who has not sufficiently worked through his or her need to rescue a person, and instead takes advantage of the patient's vulnerability by making promises or proclamations of solution or salvation, is certainly acting upon an unresolved countertransference.

In sum, Ricœur tells us, we can never fully discern the nature of the transcendent. We can, however, approach the transcendent through the capacity of the human psyche to participate in the epigenesis of a symbol. Epigenesis refers to Ricouer's method of interpreting a symbol. A real symbol, for Ricœur, points back into historical origin and is forward-moving, or prospective. The ascending dialectic of the ego with the symbol leads toward "a teleology of consciousness" (Ricœur, 1970, pp. 528, 548), a concept quite similar to Jung's understanding of the *telos* of a symbol: it points.

A teleology of consciousness, like epigenesis, also refers to the forward-moving aspect of our relationship to the transcendent with the idea that there is some plan, some continuity, some fulfillment of divine purpose that is specifically ours to meet in our internal history. Therefore, there is an intentionality or purpose to how the transcendent interrupts the immanent again and again, combining human spirit with divine spirit in dialectical motion. This "both-and" method translates into a dynamic, synthetic movement backward into personal and primordial history, and forward into potentiality where pivotal religious experiences break through.

This back-and-forth purposive movement of the epigenesis of a symbol is helpful in understanding projective identification and encouraging the value of its forward-moving potential, in contrast to just becoming stuck in it (the negative aspect of projective identification).

Applying this to a clinical example, let's say, of Po-Mo cyborg chic, which involves body piercing, we might begin analytically with the image and affect surrounding a patient's pierced navel that emulates the pop star Madonna's erotic persona. We amplify this back to a negative mother complex where, in the space of illusory and budding sexual instinct, what might have fused as a body-soul conjunction of eros and aggression, gets pierced, linked by a metal ring to the fleshly center in the psyche's attempt to hook a historical mother who maintains psychic equilibrium even in crushing her daughter's aliveness. Projectively, the daughter longs to reunite with this historical source, to recapture in some bodily way the massive libidinal thrust, the eros that she has sacrificed, now represented in the way she pierces herself as a sign of her suffering love.

As she incorporates images of this lost maternal figure, as her former images break and are redefined, as the energy flows back into life and symbol, she discovers a new mother in the figure of the Magdalene, a prostitute and whore, but a Holy whore, a Wholly Other, who leads her *back* into pregenital eros but also *forward* into sacred existence as the symbol thrusts into life the lost spirit of the deep feminine, the spirit of matter and nature.

The patient's task then becomes one of holding herself open to the ambivalence of the symbol and the prospective thrust of piercing—a whore as mother, as a mother who is both profane and sacred archetypally, as perhaps the sacred whore who is dedicated to the gods. All this begins with her projective identification onto a pop star and her yearning for unity or unitary reality, accompanied with the seeking together, of patient and analyst, for whom there are pivotal religious experiences to interpret, images to be formed and broken.

In such an example, Ricœur's point would be that we cannot throw things out just because we cannot connect with them in a rational way. Sometimes our images get broken, smashed. A gap or breach of continuity may occur when strange and Wholly Other otherness calls upon us. Breakage is part of the journey. This inbreaking, breakdown, or breakthrough, this interruption of strange otherness impels us in any case to attempt to discern the meaning that meets us in the encounter of radical otherness.

Without symbolic value, it becomes difficult to work through projections. Culturally, we desperately lack circulation between both directed (secondary) and nondirected (primary) process. One without the other leads to dogmatism, regardless on which side of the sociopolitical fence we sit. Someone, or some group, is inevitably oppressed or left out for being different, for being other.

Any extremes, emphasizing either too much primary process, where we meet with the flow of unconscious life and affective impulses in their most raw and elemental form, or too much secondary process, the reality principle, can leave us with unfleshed symbolism where anything goes (Freud, 1964, pp. 162–64).

It is all so easy to see in our culture how the predominance of the rational in a post-Enlightenment world has at best given us great gifts of medicine and science. At the same time, the arts have become autonomous and fragmentary. The dictates of anti-authority reign, and the academy is disintegrating. Consumerism intermediates. History and tradition have been dissolved, in many instances. Such cultural one-sidedness is what Ricœur is warning us about when the transformation of reality into images on a horizontal (or immanent) plane dominates.

CENTER OR CIRCUMFERENCE?

Culturally, we suffer collectively from a "fateful epistemological turn" where the symbolic has been objectified, emptied of much of its value. Objectification pertains to how we reify the symbol of the supernatural, investing popular idols, things, and objects with reality. The archetypal nature of the psyche, from a Jungian point of view, is comprised of intrinsic polarities or opposites. It has become difficult, however, for some in our modern world even to find the interior opposite, the genuine unconscious otherness necessary to live a symbolic life. As Jungian analyst and cultural critic Roman Lesmeister claims, even evil has lost its symbolic value:

> There is an increasing escape from evil. All dark matter that was kept in the individual, all that was hidden, oppressed and repressed has been brought forth in the name of Enlightenment for no other reason

than simply because it is spectacular. As a result, the minute it becomes public, it disappears. It is deprived of its content. Genuine experience is no longer important. Everything is pre-digested. The collective modes of experiencing have become a way of projective identification where the psyche is projected in the form of an image that it becomes identified with. But, at the end of the day, we don't experience the image and it remains void. As a result, evil disappears. How can we integrate our shadow if we haven't got one? (Lesmeister, 1998, p. 10)

Lesmeister feels that we do not have enough tools with which to reconcile this inflation. Our projective images have become a new kind of reality, substituting for the validity of our own dream images. Even if we engage with our images, he asks, how can we be sure that the psyche of dreams is not just referring to itself? "What good now are the myths and images of evil? How are they useful" (Ibid., p. 12)?

What we would hope for to preserve the wisdom of the psyche is a consciousness more liberated from the confines of objectification. Instead, the deconstruction of absolutes and essences has tended to replace the symbolic with two extreme orthodoxies: the orthodoxy of fundamentalism and the orthodoxy of social justice ideologies. Each exhibits a mode of exclusionary intolerance of what it defines as Other. The orthodoxy of fundamentalism adheres to scriptural literalism to the exclusion of its symbolic meaning. Social justice ideologies in their zeal substitute correct thinking for freedom of thought. Upon imbibing the "correct hermeneutic" of the culture (Horne, 1998, p. 22), the hoped-for experience of unadulterated subjectivity soon gets swallowed up into one of the forms of hegemony against which such ideologies had protested in the first place.

This rise of opposition to "ideal forms, universal claims," or categories of mind *existing behind* experience (Young-Eisendrath, 1997, p. 22; Horne, 1998, p. 27), eliminates the transcendent, the Other needed intrinsically in the development of soul and symbol. The result, ironically, is a too-immanent position that is overly focused upon development and fixated upon process.

PRIMARY OR SECONDARY PROCESS?

In his own years of breakdown and breakthrough, Jung experienced what he came to call nondirected thinking—what we call in the psychoanalytic world "primary process." In primary process, or non-directed thinking, we are engaged with our own very subjective language of affect, instinct, and image, as well as the objective process of the unconscious. Jung contrasts nondirected thinking with what he calls directed thinking (secondary process). In directed thinking, our conscious rationality dominates (Jung, 1956, pp. 16, 29). Now, there is nothing wrong with either form of thinking or process unless we have become totally one-sided to the point of eliminating the opposite form.

Jung emphasized that nondirected thinking (secondary process) is particularly susceptible to the reductive movement of objectification and depersonalization that we encounter in today's culture. Because of the predominance of directed thinking, projective images often dominate. As a culture, we are becoming very caught up in rejecting anything that resonates with "universal truth" or unifying knowledge. This is not to say that there certainly are historical reasons for deconstructing certain hegemonies, the negative effects of colonization, or any force or power that has reduced the dignity and integrity of human nature by forceful means or oppression.

Yet, psychologically speaking, there is a tremendous price to pay that accompanies deconstructive efforts that portend toward a forced and artificial equality of psychological development and the freedom to individuate within nonartificial restraints. We have put many social constructs in place with the intent to help the oppressed. Ironically (painfully so), this just puts the individual's psyche back into the torture of restriction and expectation that perhaps it is not ready to embrace. Once again, we are not respecting the specificity and uniqueness of another person's growth and psychological development.

Such culturally mandated actions, which contribute to breadth in contrast to psychological depth, produce unincarnated mush in contrast to enfleshed soul and symbol.

Although Oprah and Jerry Springer may offer inexplicably epiphanal experiences for some in the space of television illusion, we need also to look to where our projective identifications lead. Part of the difficulty with projective identification is that it becomes reification (investing popular idols, things, and objects with reality) in that we *are* trying to project ourselves into something larger in order to experience what is Wholly Other, what is unifying, but we somehow miss the prospective, forward-moving, and symbolic value of the ways in which we projectively identify.

Part of the reason for our missing the symbolic value is due to what I will speak to in the next chapter as fear and/or resistance to emotions and images of depth. We end up merged in identification with objects. Or, at the other extreme, we become extremely bored (a phrase I hear all too often in therapeutic sessions). Our psychic energy becomes withdrawn. Culturally, this means we remain rather narcissistically immature when we could be pursuing with fuller ego consciousness nondirected thinking and libidinal desire at more archaic, primordial, and deeper levels.

THE SELF-FIELD

The Self-field is profoundly described by Jung, Neumann, and Ulanov. As we and/or the patient come to relate to the Self through the Self-field in the analytic setting, the transcendent is experienced directly and immediately. We see its expression particularly in the transcendent function between the analyst and patient in the transference and countertransference (cf. Ulanov, 1997).

In the clinical setting, the Self directs all people into different combinations of relationship. The goal is that the patient comes into his/her own reality, and the Self engineers the relationship to it (Ibid., pp. 121–23). A field is created between the two people in the room that focuses upon the patient's reality and images of the Self.

The Self expresses itself through symbols. The Self-symbol is an analogue in the psychological realm (*complexio oppositorum* in Jung's terms) to the universal conjunction that I have illustrated, through Boehme and Jung's example, to be a reality that exists beyond the psyche as a predifferentiated state of being, a preexistent ground. In other words, the Self-symbol would in some way indicate the opposites existing together in a oneness. Even though a distinctness of opposition might still be evident in some form of image, the opposites would be for the most part in peaceful coexistence and working together toward creative synthesis. The basic harmony of original unity is what we remember in the experience of unitary reality when we encounter the radical otherness of the abyss/Pleroma/*Ungrund*, in the images and symbols of our own experience.

In the clinical example that follows, I address the presence of the soul and its archetypal source, particularly through dreams as they appear in clinical practice. The psyche produces what we need to work with toward the maturation and individuation of an individual as the soul evolves toward the embodied knowledge of its birthright and purpose—unitary reality.

8

TRAUMA, DREAMS, AND
RESISTANCE TO OTHERNESS

T HIS CHAPTER FOCUSES upon a clinical illustration, drawing from a six-year treatment with a woman in her thirties. Here, I illustrate the unfolding of unitary reality, or oneness, in her psyche. The emphasis is upon the difference it makes in a person's life to begin to engage in the ego-Self relationship, even though, admittedly, this relationship is a lifelong task.

In presenting this case material, I address three clinical issues that I identified in chapter 1 which I believe are germane to understanding otherness in terms of analytical psychology and clinical practice. These three issues will essentially parallel the three layers of otherness I have identified as projection/introjection, primordial, and radical otherness.

The first issue is a person's resistance to the depth of his or her own experience, especially when he or she is engaged with spontaneous images and symbols of the unconscious. Though people may appear to engage an image, often, in reality, they are not fully engaged. We see this in terms of *relationship* in the consulting room. Many people cannot see how their inner images reveal a failure in living their images interpersonally. For instance, images may appear in the transference in terms of a person's inner psychic life, but the person resists a full experience of the interpersonal encounter with the therapist. Usually, this resistance replicates what is missing in the patient's relationship to his or her partner, spouse, child, or an unresolved issue with a parent. A denial of experience seems to be operating.

The second issue that is quite obvious in the clinical setting is the difficulty of the patient to accommodate the tension of diverse ways of knowing. Even with the advent of depth psychology, where deep engagement with primordial layers of the unconscious has become more tenable, our current cultural tugs-of-war (for example, this group is "in," that group is "out") attest to the difficulty of holding opposing, or paradoxical ways of experiencing otherness in creative tension.

Third, we seem to have developed a sturdy distrust of the idea of a self in continuous relation to spirit, what I have defined earlier as an ego-Self axis. Despite the presence of a deep, direct experience, many patients find it hard to attribute gut-level passion to anything other than what is self-referential—by which I mean all knowledge is contextual and created by the ego in relation to what is known, in contrast to unknown. I would like to think that self-referential, and even interpersonal categories, do not exhaust the field of depth psychology.

Regarding otherness, I have made some distinctions, each with a corresponding layer. We can think of the first layer of otherness as that of the "me" or "not me" level in human terms. I have identified this layer as the ego's view of inner psychological contents including the projection level of otherness. Then there is the "not me" level of otherness, which I have referred to as the *primordial level* of the unconscious. Esther Harding, for example, distinguishes between the "I" of the human mind and the "not I" of the archetypal layer of existence that, although felt as within, refers to a transcendent presence beyond the human but is still of the psyche (Harding, 1965, p. 30ff.).

In another sense, radical otherness refers to something actual and real, an actuality that gives meaning to existence rather than being simply a layer or part of existence such as the psyche or society. At this level, otherness can be conceived of as "not me" in beyond-human terms; not, as Harding says, as a layer of the unconscious, but as something larger that holds both persons in the space of relationship, gives them the container for mutuality and transformation, but is an actual *source* of healing. Spirit at this layer of existence pertains to what is transcendent, ultimate, and inbreaking.

Jungian psychology emphasizes a process of resolution to our conflicts by attending to dreams or waking fantasies of otherness. In this process, we may encounter all kinds of otherness—contrasexual, cast-off, and numinous—as it is experienced by ego, the otherness that we often rationalize out of experience or ignore. The idea is to strike up an inner conversation with the contents of the psyche we meet.

A third factor emerges in this conversation, which Jung calls the "transcendent" function. Jung tells us that when we converse with the otherness we meet, a symbol begins to unfold in pictorial, tactile images that represent a synthesis of the opposing elements and a resolution to the conscious conflict (Jung, 1921, par. 825). Actively to sustain the conscious-unconscious tension between diverse pairings of otherness means, for Jung, to live a symbolic life. Sustaining this inner conversation produces symbols that are personal and specific, but also point toward an archetypal source.

An archetype, as I have identified it, is a presence, a psychic center linked to instinct and characterized by numinosity, autonomy, and unconsciousness. Archetypes are so forceful in our experience that they may lead us toward a total reorientation of our conscious position. In the course of such an inner dialogue, we really get to know our cultural specificity and, I would argue, a strong sense of our transcendent origins as well.

The three issues above, then—resistance to the depths of experience, an inability to house the tensions of diverse experiences of otherness, and distrust of a self in continuous relation to spirit (ego-Self axis, or ego-Self sphere)—are the themes I illustrate in this case. I will trace the various levels of otherness as these exist in the transference and are reflected through the symbol-making activity of the transcendent function.

I will continue to ask: How does the Self bring to consciousness a fuller experience of radical otherness through the human psyche in a way that connects an individual to his or her source? How do we continue to identify and relate to what is ineffable in our experience, but beyond the human psyche?

Jungian analyst Ann Ulanov is particularly helpful in addressing case material from two basic approaches to clinical method: (1) the reductive method, by which we analyze unconscious projection back to its historical antecedents relating dream figures to actual objects, which returns us to the ego's point of view, and (2) the synthetic method, which "conducts us to the Self's point of view (Ulanov, 1999a, p. 121). Under each of my three levels of otherness, the reductive method will be obvious until more primordial contents of the collective unconscious begin to break through, leading the ego into a painful but redemptive abyss that is engineered by the Self (Ibid.).

LAURA

Laura, whose name has been changed, was a thirty-six year old single woman of Irish descent who came to see me for therapy in the early 1990s. Employed as a waitress, she was pursuing a career as an actress. Her presenting issues included her inability to succeed in both acting and relationships with men.

In our first meeting, Laura sat defensively stiff, eyeballing me from her chair across the room. Her gaze felt impersonal, disconnected. I felt induced to initiate something to get her to talk, but my concentration felt divided. I felt unrelated, alone, surrounded only by the stark brown walls of my dimly lit office. Over the next few weeks, I began to see why Laura had developed such a tough and protective exterior, one that induced such feelings in me.

In Laura's own words (with her permission):

Before ten, I don't remember much. After twelve, I was drunk or on uppers, downers, and LSD. Until I was thirty, I numbed myself so I could survive. Had to get sober 'cause I almost killed someone. Tried to strangle a woman who pissed me off. The only reason I didn't kill her was 'cause I blacked out. I used to think the reason I got angry so much was 'cause of my drinking. Since I've been sober, I've had even bigger anger, like when I threw my roommate's cat across the room.

Can't seem to stay in a relationship either. I lived with a guy and did drugs for six years when I was in my twenties. Probably had something to do with my dad. My dad laid bricks when he wasn't drunk. We moved around a lot cause he was always losing his jobs. Sometimes he wouldn't come home for a couple days. When he was home, he'd just be drunk and hitting me. My brother and my sister didn't get it; just me.

My dad finally went sober after ending up in jail for the eight-billionth time. 'Cause of my family, I just don't connect. I don't want to deal with anger like my dad. But I don't want to be numb either. I came back East to be an actress, but I keep putting everything off, auditions, classes, and all. I've been waiting tables ever since. I worked with a therapist, but I hated it. She wanted me to talk to a chair. We just couldn't communicate. I never had any relationship with my mom either.

Everything's just so screwed up. I don't feel good about myself, like ashamed of everything. And angry. I'm angry all the time. I feel like a walking time bomb. I don't want to keep running from everything. God, I hate this. I hate for anyone to see me cry.

Because Laura could recall few specific memories of her childhood, exploring dreams gave us important clues to the severity of early trauma. I have always thought that Laura's presenting dream indicated her potential. In it, she and a woman identified as her sister or her mother, were traveling in a green VW (the family car), and they came to a fork in the road where there were two different ways to go. Laura took one of the roads by herself.

Over the course of our six years together, I encountered a variety of others involving all three layers of otherness and a multiplicity of images and emotions from wrath-fire and tortured flesh to something analogous to Boehme's "liberty-blue." Many characters populated Laura's inner drama, appearing in her rich dream life. The most important of these was a twinlike character, sometimes a sister and sometimes a male counterpart who bore physical resemblance to her. There was a predominance of antilibidinal figures, such as demon lovers and torturers.

Antilibidinal refers to a form of ego splitting. The patient is viewed as having an internal closed system of self-persecution and an internal world of bad objects (cf. for instance, Harold Guntrip 1968, p. 212). In this split of the ego into parts, one part seeks to fulfill libidinal needs and another part turns against its other half with what might be otherwise useful aggression in life. Ironically, the antilibidinal ego serves the personality as a protective defense.

We see this defensive structure in action especially throughout the early years of treatment. The antilibidinal ego effectively sabotages the positive efforts made by a person toward life and often does so with a sort of cruel and vehement violence toward the more vulnerable part of the self.

Even though the term comes from a different school of psychology from Jung's, that of Ronald Fairbairn and Harold Guntrip, the antilibidinal defense is of some import in working through the first two layers of otherness I have described: projection/introjection, and the primordial layer of the psyche. This notion is of further import in the context of abyss and descent since the antilibidinal ego actually gathers strength as the personality engages with the deeper layers of unconscious content and moves toward what E. Neumann has called "the borderline experience of the psychoid layer of archetypal reality." Likewise, Boehme, totally outside any analytic notions, mapped out of his encounter a similar ruthless and wrathful reality that he called "abyss of the dark world," and as he proceeded further inward, "eternal hell of devils" (1911, pp. 45, 60). For Boehme, "the soul needs burn thus a while" until spirit can enter.

Even though the antilibidinal figures were predominant for Laura, another, more diffuse figure, a kindly grandmother was also present at times as a quality of feeling. What appeared to be most absent was a mother figure, although in her presenting dream Laura indicated that the sister figure could also be her mother. She was not sure, and certainly the longings were present in affect form.

A striking image that emerged from extensive and intensive dreamwork was what I call Laura's door. This image manifested itself in a number of forms. At the beginning of our work there were two large wooden doors in a dream, one that was closed to her and one that she herself closed. She was shut out, but also self-isolated. This image also took the form in another dream of a sliding glass door with the sister figure behind it, out of reach, inaccessible. Later, in actual life, it became a glass partition separating Laura from me during her participation in an observation group at the clinic where I was seeing her as a patient and also completing my four-year residency.

A breakthrough in our third year of work together occurred when Laura began to equate me with the antilibidinal as well as the sister characters in her dreams. She used me, her analyst, to hold *both* of these opposites, the positive sister and the negative attacker(s). When finally, during the course of a few sessions of this same year, she linked me in the transference with the negative qualities of her inner torturer and also the sister who was trying to reach her, a turning point occurred. Laura needed to witness her inner opposites as outer, in me, to be able to separate from them in order to be reunited to them and to relate to them in a new way, but she first experienced her opposites as projected into me. I, as other, carried them for her. From this watershed in treatment, the process of healing split-off parts truly began.

At this point, I would like to recap the three clinical issues I raised at the beginning, in the form of a continuum, to interpret the progress of my work with Laura in the context of unitary reality.

1. A resistance or openness to the depths of experience
2. An inability or ability to house the tensions and contradictions of diverse experiences of otherness
3. A distrust or trust of a continuous ego-Self axis

Behind the Glass Door: Resistance to the Depths of Experience

An illustration of Laura's resistance to the depths of her own experience can be seen in the following dream, which she brought in the latter half of our first year.

> Dad, Grandpa, and I were in the field of a huge stadium watching a sports thing. We had a duplex apartment house on the other side of the stands. We were watching a tornado coming and I stayed really close

to the house. My sister was in a huge dark room just out of the main room with a sliding glass door. She told me to "get out, don't bother me." It was dark and windy but nobody blew away. I was both excited and scared about the wind. Everyone cheered after it left. My sister still did not want to come in.

Laura associated the sister behind the sliding glass door as that part of her that does not want to be bothered in real life because she is "very angry about being neglected." Along with her self-sufficient, aggressive outer self, there seemed to be another self split from conscious awareness, a self that had gone into hiding. In a negative form, we see otherness in terms of the shadow aspect of the personal psyche, using Jung's term. We scapegoat and cast off parts of our self that we do not like, cannot own, or find distasteful.

Laura's "get out" ensured that any interpretations were ignored or forgotten, as if they could not get through the glass partition to the girl beyond it. The image that arose for me, in response to the girl behind the sliding glass door, was that of a watchful hound, a Cerebrus that kept at bay all who approached too closely.

Then one day, when in treatment, something changed, but it was not in Laura's external self. Significantly, it was the sister behind the glass door. Laura came into treatment one afternoon, dressed entirely in black leather, and announced that she had been sick with a sore throat for seven days. She then related a dream in which she and a sisterlike figure had fought. The sisterlike figure was trying to connect with her, but she (Laura) did not want to participate. Laura was glad to maintain the separation, but the sister was struggling to make contact with Laura as if the sister's defensive "get out" had faded into a need for relationship with Laura.

As an example of Laura's progressive opening to the depths of experience in and around this time in our work, I would like to relate a "turning point" session that illustrates the change I have referred to. After feeling angry for two weeks, Laura came in and spoke of her longing to have been a little girl who could skip and play alongside her father, recalling instead how her father had shot the tires out in the family car. Lost in a train of images, she described a room from childhood that had brown walls, which I found interesting given the context of my consulting room having walls of the same color: "I never wanted to go home to this room," she said. "I wanted to go to my grandmother's house instead." During this session, Laura presented a dream in which a child is caught up in a magical illusion that appears to be real. As Laura associated to this dream, she remembered that she had once had a book called *The Princess and the Woodcutter's Daughter* (Bromhall, 1955). In this story, a lonely princess longs for a sister figure who could teach her to play and a warm home where everyone would be gathered around a table. The princess escapes from her castle through a small door, falls into a pool of water in the forest, is taken home by the Woodcutter's daughter, and experiences what it is like to live outside a fortress wall. When she finally returns home to the castle, a new baby has been born to her parents, which the princess relates to as a good thing because she was so lonely for a sister figure, someone who could reflect and mirror her. In the context of relating this story, Laura also remembered that her mother had never read aloud to her.

I was particularly caught by these words. Something urged me to pick up the dream I had written down as she presented it and to read it back to her. I read slowly, as if I was reading a story to a small child.

> There was a couple. They weren't a couple at first until the female figure read a book the male figure gave her—some sort of magical book, but it was not about magic. Then the story came alive somehow.
>
> This couple had a child and the mother left it with the father while she went away. The father didn't watch the child very well, and the child became fascinated with a character from the book. The magic became real. The child left with this character. It wasn't children's magic. It was dark and scary but the child went anyway. When the mother came back and her child was gone, she fought with the man.

I had become accustomed to perceiving Laura as a fighter, a fairly aggressive force with which to contend. When I looked up from reading her this story, however, I saw before me a little girl. Her face was soft, her cheeks flushed, her eyes large as buttons and welling up with big tears. It was as if Laura had arrived at some forgotten place of sanctuary from long ago, as if, for a moment, the little girl (the sister!) behind the glass door was sitting in the chair in front of me, accessible, and real, open to and clearly touched by a depth of experience I had not witnessed in our treatment thus far.

Laura was able to pick up a mirrored reflection in the transference of my carrying the otherness of the split-off sister, and to witness at the same time, through a mirrored reality, my mirroring her little girl, the manifestation of her own sacrificed vulnerability. She could receive it without also destroying it and to know in her feeling, which means also in the body, what it was like to have the sister-self knit together in contrast to the ego's one-sided view: "Get out, I can take care of myself, thank you very much."

THE TENSIONS OF DIVERSE EXPERIENCES OF OTHERNESS

Basically, I have described three layers of otherness. Clearly, splitting had occurred in Laura as a defensive reaction against a noxious early environment, and the objects that gave her the most trouble had been internalized or introjected in order to control them.

In the initial years of treatment, it was clear in her dreams that Laura was tormented by antilibidinal characters that usually took the form of dangerous male figures, images that Jung would speak of as negative animus figures portraying a negative connection of the ego to the Self. In one dream, during the first year, a dream man accompanied Laura through a murky swamp, and tempted her with heroin.

A dangerous male figure continued to appear in her dreams as one who had invaded Laura's house, her interior. He watched her and looked through cracks in the hallway. In one dream, a "violent crime" was done by a lover who had hurt, beat, and raped her, finally causing her "music to disappear." Music seemed to represent for Laura a place of original refuge where sets of opposites could exist simultaneously with the potential for symbolic value, as exemplified in the following dialogue from one of our sessions.

K: Were you ever allowed to have your feelings without being told to stop crying all the time?

L: Well, definitely not a display of any sort of emotion. That was a big "no no." 'Cause then, in my mom's eyes, everyone would see how not together we were.

K: So, no one saw your feelings?

L: No, definitely not. 'Cause feelings were not allowed inside or outside the house, period.

K: What did you do with them?

L: I don't really know, honestly. Just didn't have them. Well, I started drinking when I was twelve. Before that, I think I just shut up.

K: Where did your feelings go when you shut up?

L: They didn't go anywhere. I just pretended I didn't have them. It's hard to remember. I think one thing was that I just sat and listened to music.

K: By yourself?

L: Uh-huh. And watched movies, like John Wayne. I was so into westerns.

K: What about them?

L: Everything was just laid out. There was the good guy and the bad guy. You knew who the good guy was 'cause he wore a white hat and who the bad guy was 'cause he had a black hat, and it seemed like there was always the hero that saved the day. It was just sort of a fantasy. You knew that the good guy was always gonna win. I like those fantasies.

K: You're having a lot of feeling about that right now.

L: Yeah. It's the good-guy thing. (Laughs. Cries.) Everything was always so confusing in my house. What was going on was never what was really going on. I mean, I always had to pretend. It was just all fake. I mean, I could never feel what I was feeling entirely. I was always wrong no matter what the situation: "Don't be such a baby. Don't cry so much."

I remember one time throwing a fit around my aunt and uncle. My dad was really drunk, and he was gonna drive home. And I was terrified to get in the car cause I knew he was drunk. And, I didn't want to die. I was like eight or nine. And all the adults said, "Oh, don't be so silly. He's fine.'" And they put us in the car. And I remember knowing that he couldn't drive 'cause he couldn't even talk when drunk, let alone drive with three kids and a wife in the car. And he'd be turning around yelling, not watching the road, swerving. And I was terrified. But everybody said, "Oh, you're fine."

So, I wasn't allowed to sit there and be mad, or be scared, or anything. "He's fine. Can't you see he's fine? What's wrong with you?" they'd ask. My brother, being completely shut down, didn't say anything. He obediently got into the car. My sister was young and hadn't a clue. Just situations like that all the time. *Don't be so sad. He's fine. Everything's fine*: And I knew damn well it's not fine!

K: So you had a lot of people telling you what your feelings were and what they weren't?

L: Yeah.

Not only in Laura's internal world but also in the external world, projection was visible as a layer of otherness that was carried for her in the choices she made in life that represented still unconscious content. I noticed that as we engaged her more-vulnerable feelings, a theme of black-versus-white became increasingly more apparent (the Westerns) in and around the third year of treatment and before the turning point I mentioned earlier. In one dream, she became two people, black and white.

She took two babies up a tree and bound both with ropes to the tree branches. Then, the babies grew into teenagers. Laura associated one of the babies with her "blank period," referring to her inability to recall many memories before the age of ten. I thought in terms of H. Guntrip, who has a particularly helpful understanding of ego splitting.

In this dream, we might consider the two babies as the splitting of the libidinal ego and the banishing of weak, infantile needs, where "very early in life a human being tends to become cruelly divided against himself and becomes a self-frustrating and at times even a self-destroying creature" (Guntrip, 1969, p. 189). Laura could not contain the opposites, the two branches, the two babies, internally. The image of the blank period baby resonated with the way Laura had dealt with oral libidinal needs by numbing herself with drugs and alcohol.

Also, when at one point I noted to Laura how she wore either all black or all white clothing to sessions, rarely a color, she hesitantly shared what she felt was an embarrassing pattern: her propensity for dating men of color. Being Caucasian, for Laura a choice that rather than expressing a celebration of difference, seems instead to sustain an inner mechanism of splitting in her external life without addressing the deeper causes. Laura's antilibidinal ego was thus acted out in a projective way of relating as well as acting internally in her psyche, as self-attack. and therefore these relationships never lasted.

Laura's inability to house this intrapsychic other led to more anger. Repeatedly, she had images of something large squishing something small, accompanied by feelings that were "big and overwhelming, and the inner voices negative." She feared "going over the edge and tearing my room apart" and then missed her sessions for two weeks, sleeping through her scheduled time. Upon returning, she said that she was "frustrated that I had not yet fixed her." When we explored this, Laura looked straight into me and cried deeply, saying "you see too much of me," meaning that she felt I had seen what she called the weak, pathetic part of herself. "I want an angel," she said. "I want hope. I'm pissed at you because you offer none of this."

ABYSS OF NOTHINGNESS

I always wanted to call you mama,
That word doesn't fit our relationship.
Mama is warm and loving.
Pressed and primping,
You make the inherited face
In the mirror
To look outside of you.
Don't look too close,
Or those lines can turn white,
Lines on the highway.
Escaping on the run
From the man
Or the bill-collector—
You dragged us out into the night,
Escapees, luggage in hand,
To the nearest motel
Lulling us into false safety,
Or another whim-fantasy,
For a night of restful
Sleep, sleep, sleep.

(A poem Laura brought to
a session in our third year)

In the months following, still around the third and fourth year of treatment, Laura felt terribly exposed in terms of both vulnerability and in terms of making conscious some of the inner workings of her brutal antilibidinal ego. She began to suffer from headaches, neck and shoulder pain, and said that she feared an impending illness or injury.

Another theorist who is particularly helpful while working from the reductive perspective in the early to middle years of treatment, D. W. Winnicott, would explain symptoms such as these as an organized defense that keeps separate the conflict in the psyche and is often at the level of primitive agony. Winnicott (1958) and M. Sidoli (1993) suggest that "primal" and "irrepresentable" symptoms may be used as "defenses of the self" preventing infantile contents from acquiring symbolic mental representation. Sidoli is also relevant among Jungian theorists in the context of working with developmental injury. Laura's longings became evermore visceral:

L: I swear, I've had this stomachache for two days. I don't know if I have the stomach flu, or if thinking about all this is making my stomach hurt. I don't want it to eat away at me and get cancer, if I can't say what's on my mind. I just don't know what the fear is. It's so huge. I just think that the bottom line is that—again—it's the same old thing. I think it's the idea of someone saying "see you later" because of what *I feel*. That's the bottom line.

K: Can you say more about the fear?

L: I just feel lonely and empty and sad, like there's something wrong with me. It's just that *huge empty hole that's always been there*. And I'm afraid that it's always going to be there, and that there's never

going to be anything to put in it. And I'm not so
sure if just loving myself and doing good things for
myself is enough. I mean, I know being able to love
myself has filled part of the hole but there's more to
it than just that.

K: What would that be?

L: You know, as wrong as this sounds, I just think I
want someone to love me back. That's it. *To be* there.
You know, *to want to be there.* I feel so embarrassed
when I talk about this. It seems like such a ridiculous
thing to be sad about.

Along with the persecutory figures in her dreams and
memory, Laura more consistently and consciously could
identify her deep longings for an angel of hope. In retro-
spect, I see that this marked growth in terms of Laura's
ability to house the tensions and contradictions of otherness in her psyche.

At the same time, in the transference I could feel
her need that I be physically and emotionally present to
the intense fears arising in her. In an induced countertransference, in which feelings or images are induced in
the analyst that are not part of his or her usual subjective, affective and/or bodily realm, I experienced a certain
amount of angst in light of what I anticipated this yet-
to-be-named presence might require of me. The induced
countertransference signaled the size of the suffering that
Laura might have to endure, and I could feel my own
defenses rising in light of whatever it was that felt so big
and yet unknown.

Attending to my own defenses was important in
this transition. The analyst cannot get in the way of the
Self's original plan for the person. The analyst's counter-

transference to the Self affects the field and different levels of entry into the field (Ulanov, 1999a, pp.10–12). The more open and receiving the analyst can be toward this objective presence, the greater the possibility for the patient to live into the wholeness of unitary reality, which has to do with housing the opposites on the road to individuation.

An analyst has often gone into the profession (at least in my speculation) because he or she has experienced unitary reality in some way. The fact of this experience enables the therapist to offer a special kind of holding in the clinical setting since he or she has experienced this depth of being in his or her own struggle to unite the opposites and has come to trust the Self's greater knowledge and potentiality. I think that we analysts are often motivated to restore in others the original unity that has been experienced in some way in ourselves.

At the same time, we cannot get in the way of what is coming into view in terms of the Self for the patient, even if this means traveling alongside this individual into the vortex of the abyss. At the juncture of primordial otherness, the patient's ego gives way to the archetypal transference object, the object that expresses through the images and feelings of transference the deeper, radical layer of otherness as projected onto the perceived reality of the therapist (Ulanov, 1997, p. 121). The analyst cannot predict in advance what the archetypal layer will look or feel like. We can predict that the encroaching Self will be something that neither the patient nor the analyst has witnessed in the field between them, even though we may have gotten hints along the way. What we can anticipate is that the Self will bear some combination of the opposites, for instance, an admixture of the innocent child and the ruthless antilibidinal sentry in Laura's case.

The analyst's job is to be present to this reality and to be a sort of midwife to the birthing of the third thing that incarnates. As Ulanov tells us, the transference shifts from the objective level to the subjective, from the level of reductive analysis in which dream figures are related to their corresponding actual objects, to the level of synthetic analysis that brings the objective contents into combination with the subjective (Ibid., p. 120).

Toward the end of treatment, an important dream further helped Laura contain the contradictory parts of herself. She dreamed of the death of a pilot she associated with her boyfriend at the time (a musician). The pilot died, but seeing that she was sad he came to her house as a "ghost in the next room." He was accompanied by a group of her friends who came and danced with her into the night and made her laugh.

The antilibidinal pilot was no longer in charge. Laura's split between vulnerability and destructive antilibidinal aggression seemed less toxic in the figure of a ghost. Once a figure of bad magic, her torturer had metamorphosed into spirit of a sort, as if her opposites needed each other. Rather than controlling her inner world with sadomasochistic flare, the ghost-spirit had begun to relate the various parts of her inner world to their common center with a *telos* and intentionality (Kalsched, 1996, p. 130). Something had changed that had needed to change.

DISTRUST OF A CONTINUOUS EGO-SELF AXIS

Finally, I would like to offer some examples of the continuum of distrust/trust of a continuous ego-Self axis or ego-Self sphere. We can observe how the Self exists as a bridging, mediating factor between the primordial layer of otherness and radical other otherness, the "not me" in beyond-human terms. Edward Edinger tells us that if the "unconscious dynamism that seeks the center is activated without the ego's being consciously related to it, dangerous or destructive aspects appear" (1995, p. 135). In other words, when the ego is too weak and immature to relate to the central dynamism of the Self, we find distrust, even denial, of relation to something larger. Something is happening. But not yet. The "lonely one" has to gaze into the void.

With Laura, in and around the second year of her treatment, this distrust appeared in the image of a chest of drawers to which she associated "antique material." The chest of drawers had old blankets inside, and she and I mused about the possibility of her having some self-care resources in connection to the maternal because she associated the antique with the protective care of her grandmother, a very positive image for Laura. At the time, her reactive anger kept her from holding onto her vulnerable feelings, however, and she continued to lash out with a venomous tongue and sank into withdrawal.

In and around the fifth year of treatment, her distrust also took the form of a "circle of torture and pins," manifested in a dream of two women, one man, and a torturer, all of whom Laura associated as parts of herself. The torturer made the three of them walk in circles and kept asking them questions about themselves that they had to answer. It felt like an inquisition. The more they answered, the more trouble they got into. The man's arm was being cut and something was being put inside him. One woman was having straight pins put inside her vagina by the torturer. They pointed down and out, which made it difficult to walk. She walked slowly with her head down, answering questions for the torturer while walking in a circle.

Laura felt detached from the dream, but identified with the woman whose vagina was lined with pins. Strangely, she did not associate pain with her therapy. She associated walking in circles and torture with the pins and seemed cut off from feeling in her body. "You go in circles, around and around, and come again to the same thing. It feels like constant torture, questioning yourself all the time."

On the other hand, I began to note the pattern of a continuous, bridging Self unfolding in Laura's treatment in terms of images of circles, a repeated image of the antique chest of drawers, the quaternium—a symbol of wholeness and the squaring of the circle. In alchemy, known to both Boehme and Jung (1959a, par. 20), the circle represents unity, the square represents the four elements, and the quaternium, a totality of four parts (1959b, pars. 297, 397).

Interestingly, in the dream above the two women, one man, and the torturer comprise a *quaternio,* a totality of four. Torture represents the *motif,* in the alchemical *opus,* the work of individuation itself (Jung, 1983, par. 439). These images in Laura's psyche represent the mysterious ordeal that works on the arcane (unconscious, hidden, unknowable) material to transform the three into a unified one.

Here the torture of mortification, what alchemy calls the stage of *mortificatio* on the way to wholeness, is applied to the body (Ibid., par. 441). What was once experienced as desire, or desire in its representative form as the literal senses in contrast to the interior senses or senses of the soul, is separated out from its old form and symbolically killed in its obsessive, projected form (a vagina "pinned" from the inside, for example, to servicing something, to having something put inside it as a literal container, an image of shame, in contrast to a container contained, the content or soul in the service of the person or Self) in the service of the first step in the alchemical process of individuation, *unio mentalis*.

In this stage, soul is symbolically separated out (liberated) from matter. "Only separated things can reunite," Jung says. The body's affectivity and instinctuality must be transcended, but first, there must be a dissociation of the spirit-soul from the body in order to establish a spiritual position, one where the Self is born out of the otherness of the *nigredo*. The *nigredo* refers to the *prima materia*, the black mass, the chaos of the individuation process of alchemy. The *nigredo* is sometimes associated with melancholy, walking head down in Laura's dream imagery, being tortured, mortified, trapped in a "black hole" that is numb to feeling, yet full of its own life, still unconsciously so—the subjective state of depression (Ibid., par. 331). The *nigredo* is equivalent to a voluntary death and precedes the *rubedo* (Jung, 1989, par. 670ff). The *rubedo* represents the quintessence of the rose-colored blood of alchemy that cannot be held back as the self struggles to make itself manifest and threatens to overpower consciousness (Jung, 1983, par. 433).

In truth, Laura and I had come to a numbed and depersonalized center. Her therapy felt circular and tormenting in its demand for constant introspection. We were "doing" too much and needed to "be" more to allow for a mutual descent into the abyss represented symbolically by Laura's vaginal vortex.

Three circular images of transition appear in my work with Laura. As her analyst, I had provided a container and had become the other who, for some time, had carried the mystery of the transcendent function. Laura's transferential projections had symbolically represented the potential for union of her ego with an aspect of her personality that was not fully developed, which she projected into me when she saw me as sister and Self. In Jung's view, the creative actuality of the Self emerges from our longing to connect with that within us that is still unconscious.

I watched while our relationship, always important as a container, became secondary to the more intentional unfolding of Laura's psyche. First, she explained that something new was occurring by describing a magnet with its poles reversed. Thinking back on the MRI image of the great magnet, I recalled there is an archetypal field that exists that embraces both the inner and outer dimensions of the person. This archetypal field is a segment of the unitary reality.

When we begin to have glimpses of this unitary reality, we find that we cannot locate it except in images and symbols. The "knowledge" itself is suspended in the field (Neumann, 1989, p. 72). In the field, the patient and analyst are brought together into a structure of sorts as a magnet attracts radio waves or metal filings. At the same time, either can work against the pull of this field or magnet.

Where my earlier countertransference to Laura had consisted of concern about sufficient holding, this "turning around" allowed me to understand her transference as essentially archetypal. Just as it is impossible for the personal mother to provide the entire range of archetypal possibilities, so will it be for the analyst. Thus, if both patient and analyst are willing to meet the unknown, the work "turns around" from a more objective, reductive approach to external objects to a subjective one. What results is that the therapist carries both positive and negative contents for the patient in the transference. Laura could witness the original wound through the wisdom of the objective psyche as other.

She dreamed again of an antique chest of drawers, one she had purchased but could not manage to ship back to New York from the West Coast. Here again "antique" seemed to represent something more primordial, a "Grandmother," something that was seeking to connect with her with some intentionality.

Abyss of Nothingness and Fullness

What, besides being-in-relationship with me—her analyst—was at work here? It became quite clear to me that the archetypal and the primordial each has its own momentum. Watching Laura build a new ego, one that could sustain an inner conversation and suffer the opposites of the torturer and the little girl behind the glass door, both now more free to circulate into consciousness, shed light for me upon how the transcendent function works. Together, we experienced the "me" and "not me" of Laura's torturer, for instance, and the "not me" and "me" of her sister figure.

Something radically other was yet to come, however, in the swing of the pendulum back and forth between the opposites of innocence and murderous aggression.

At the same time, it was as if she had reached the dregs of the barrel. In order for unitary reality to happen when the ego's position is one-sided or in too much control, the type of suffering breakdown that I have illustrated with Boehme and Jung is needed. Not all unitary reality involves breakdown literally, but it is more a long process in which the ego gives way incrementally to a larger Self. The Self orchestrates this new center as crucial to wholeness and individuation.

Toward the end of our fifth year together, she arrived sunken and agitated with a dream she called "Mother's Day":

> There was a game of "three strikes, you're out" where people were chosen to die. Two men would throw a baseball at someone's door and stun the person, making the person numb. These men were caring but sneaking and evil. People died in the game from bleeding to death.
>
> In the dream, I was bleeding real bad from my vagina but not from my period. I was trying to hide the fact I was bleeding but the men knew. I tried to clean up the blood but left stains on the toilet. Then I tried to escape, looking for policemen to help catch the bad guys. When leaving the house, I saw a woman on the porch. The woman was dying. She had played the game and when you play, you die.

Laura associated the men and the game with her mother: "I think she's numb, unwilling to look at herself and at reality." The depersonalized numbness of Laura's dream was configured as "the game," which had become the reality of her own sexual life. She associated the game with many occasions on which she had blacked out when drunk and "didn't know what was what." Caught in a pre-symbolic, somatic identity with her mother, she could be penetrated only when her body was annihilated from feeling. As Laura claimed, "Sex was the only love for me and my sister. When you play the game, you die. Someone has to die," Laura insisted, while offering a second half of the dream:

> I was driving in a car with two girlfriends. Jennifer was driving. I had a secret and blacked out, and I couldn't remember what it was. Then Jennifer found my underwear in a cup in her car and asked me why I put it in there; and I felt really ashamed, really embarrassed.

This dream reminded Laura specifically of times she had drank and found her underwear in a cup the next day: "I felt like an ugly, bad, bad girl," associating the cup as plastic, and of "a cheap sort. But the cup also contained a secret."

Left mercilessly to "the game" of numbing, Laura had filled the gap with sexual activity. By the age of thirty-two, she could no longer remember all the sexual exploits, the repulsion, the pain of the wound, just the blank, black hole. Long before Laura's love of music had died, her mother had failed to relate with optimal responsiveness sufficient to engage Laura with an imaginal, symbolic world. This failure forestalled the possibility of housing the transcendent function creatively by which I mean being able to sustain her longings and her aggression together in a constructive synthesis that would also equate with a bodily reality. In contrast to the numbing game, here, in the dream, blood poured forth from a wound of deep feminine bodily shame.

"I lost a child at sixteen," Laura suddenly added to her dream associations. I was totally startled. She had never spoken of this. Then she added that her teenage pregnancy had been aborted, not just "lost." Here was another layer to her dream as a game where one is made numb by caring-but-sneaking men (doctors performing the abortion), the torture and inquisition of her dream, where people (babies) are chosen to die, and where babies and mothers die from bleeding to death. The blood stains now had an entirely different meaning. Her psyche had helped her ego "to gather into its own present time and experience the original experience of the primitive agony" (Hazell, 1996). There was purpose to her suffering. Now, Laura re-membered and witnessed the "otherness" of her own death. The woman sitting on the porch was both an aborting mother and Laura's detachment from her own act. Interestingly, Jennifer, a sister figure for her in real life, was now in the driver's seat.

As Laura consciously and willingly entered into continuous relationship with the otherness of her mother, her male torturer, and her sister-self, she found that her "cup" was more than a vortex of repulsion. In the game of depersonalization, she had been "chosen to die," an interesting image in light of the mortification of analysis being voluntary. Her conscious ego witnesses its own traumatized origins: "I saw a woman on the porch; she was dying." As she suffers this consciously, humbly, and without disintegrating, "something happens" that restores the music. Her wound, in relation to symbolic death was a death that empties the cup only to fill it.

The *rubedo* of Laura's bleeding is both trauma and victory. The self-sacrifice is one of moral obligation, a time of great urgency. If a person gives way to the demands of rational, external life (in the image of pins in the vagina and a torturer that Laura then could not feel) in contrast to suffering the "soul substance in the form of rose-colored blood, then the Self has lost the game as well, having overcome or destroyed the human being who should have been its vessel" (Jung, 1983, par. 433). In other words, even the torture and torturer were purposive. *It* suffers me. The eye of the eye. It longs us into being. It longs to know us that we may be known by it: the Self in Jung's terms, the redemptive, holy God, in Boehme's.

Laura did not succumb. She seemed freed from her chains of torment. At the level of spirit, Laura experienced radical otherness as "not me" in beyond-human terms in the numinous redemption of her own feminine spirit. The progression progressed from a "not me" that was me to a "not me" in terms of the opposites being carried in me, to Laura receiving and giving back from her own responsive reflectivity, her own consciousness of what was birthing inside her, spirit. The following week, Laura shared a budding image from her active imagination:

> I imagined I was the mother of a ten-year-old girl. This child carried a leather pouch filled with healing herbs to the bass player of a band.

I couldn't help thinking of Laura's "pouch," once so penetrated by pins and yet, in the crucible of the cup, in the mystery of the shed blood, emerging as a "living third thing," the "new potential…a transition to the new attitude of the transcendent function" (Jung, 1989, par. 257).

I noticed, then, another circular image of transition. Laura began wearing around her neck a silver talisman in the shape of a woman whose vagina was the striking centerpiece of the pendant. As Laura continued to grapple with the radical otherness at the layer of spirit, the roundness of the woman and the dilated opening struck me as a symbol of birthing. The alchemical *opus* is sometimes depicted in images of incubation and pregnancy. "Now," Laura claimed boldly, stroking the talisman, "I'm the *conscious* one!" Here, and in the offering of the leather pouch of healing herbs, was further integration of the personality, a bridging of the split between the maternal, the child, and the torturer. Laura called this "soul retrieval." I think she was right.

TRUST OF EGO-SELF AXIS

At the end of our fifth year, Laura had begun to write poems and stories. She began to develop the fantasy of becoming a teacher of adolescent children, saying, "I know there are many doors down a long hallway, and that the right one will open if I prepare myself." She went on to complete a college degree that had been pending for years. Before we completed our work together, she had been placed in a student-teaching position in a class of young Korean students taking English as a second language. She said that she wanted to show them word pictures and to capture them with good magic. "They are shy and withdrawn but eager to learn," she reported affectionately.

In our last year together, Laura dreamed that she was at a family reunion where many families gathered in a circle around a fire. Her role was to guide people to the group to which they belonged. This dream presented a classic symbol of wholeness—a mandala—in the shape of a large wheel of families surrounding and connected to a central fire with Laura's ego as the connecting link. Laura viscerally felt a largeness of space and described an open sky. She expressed awe and gratitude in association with a feeling of going home.

She spoke with urgency about her impending move back to her home state on the West Coast and described the home she envisioned. "There will be four rooms in green, brown, and rose, a big eating space, and a sliding glass door! Through the sliding glass door, you can *see through* to the bright, sunny ocean (blue) and the beach." She dreamed of having a beautiful little daughter and "just kissing and kissing her—all her fingers and toes." Together, she and her daughter sat in their front lawn while everyone else had a yard sale. Laura had an antique dresser, but she did not want to sell it. "Everything was fine."

Laura's psyche's juxtaposition of the circle (mandala wheel) and the square (antique dresser) is interesting in light of what Jung speaks of as the squaring of the circle. The squaring of the circle involves the breaking down of an original chaotic unity into four elements and recombining them into a higher unity. The process is "a stage on the way to the unconscious, a point of transition leading to a goal lying as yet unformulated beyond it" (Jung, 1968, par. 167). Soul and spirit begin united with each other in the alchemical process. Then the united product is separated from the body, which is analogous to a voluntary death (torturer and tortured). After a long process of purification, the combined third product of soul and spirit that arises from the ashes (body, sexuality, aliveness, the new, an impregnation of spirit) is infused back into the body (the possibility of a child). The body is the fourth. Through this process, there arises a totality of four parts into one depicted as a circle within a square.

Jung makes an important distinction regarding this transformation. "It is the arcane substance that suffers physical and mental tortures," (1963, par. 492) not the individual. In other words, *it* suffers in her, *it* is tortured, *it* passes through death and rises again. What is this *it? It* is the inner other, the Self, born out of the cauldron of transformation at the level of the abyss.

Laura could now maintain an inner conversation, represented by the mandala wheel and a quaternium of four rooms (a symbol of the Self) replete with a sliding-glass partition that both protects and separates the ego but opens at one end to the larger Self, and the Self to the transcendent as spirit. The redemption of her own feminine soul at the psychoid level of the abyss was a symbolic death that gave birth to the new, however painfully so. It was a psychological experience in which the opposites were held together as a unitary reality, a deep and direct experience of the nothingness coexisting with fullness, fullness being the potentiality of the creative generativity of the human being in relation to spirit.

When spirit of the layer beyond the psyche *exists* in us, as I have tried to demonstrate with Laura, the analyst knows that the transformation of a patient is not just a matter of having some special intuitive knowledge, nor a matter of the patient having the same. As an analyst, we might experience that "something-urged-me" feeling, like an artist who doesn't just play the notes but is in touch with the music in a deep, soul-to-soul connectedness.

In the sense of radical otherness, spirit then includes the transcendent function in the psyche. But the transcendent function and the symbol it produces point beyond to the free, limitlessness of spirit. As Ann Ulanov tells us,

> If we consciously engage the transcendent function in our psyches, we may experience Transcendence at the source, working in and through us. The Transcendent functions in our lives all the time, whatever we choose to call it—God, or the unknown, or the holy, or the numinous, or the all-in-all. (Ulanov, 1996, pp. ix, xi)

We can ground our approach as analysts in this freedom, even if initially the patient fears or resists the fact of immediate experience, the depth of experience, or a continuity of experience. We ground it by intuiting, grasping, and acknowledging all that exists and passes through consciousness—both the existential *and* the transcendent.

The Birth of Symbol as a Green VW

When the way is cleared of introjective and projective layers of relating, spirit is free to conjoin the personal and the transcendent, and subject and object distinctions are transcended. We find ourselves engaged in an active encounter with all that is other within us, which eventually leads us beyond being a fragmented part into becoming a particular part of a larger whole where community becomes an extension of one's Self. Psychologically, this involves suffering all the opposites, as I have shown with Laura.

My work with Laura has persuaded me that the space in-between two persons opens to otherness, and spirit can become a truly virginal matrix where the life-giving essence of a small girl behind a paralyzing wall of glass can not only survive but also flourish.

The day I met Laura, as discussed, she presented a dream of the green VW on the highway. Laura rode in the front seat with her sister (or mother) driving until they came to two roads. There, Laura branched off and took one road, her sister-mother, the other.

In our last year, Laura dreamed of riding as a solo driver who comes to the edge of the sea. In her words: "I am driving down a long road by myself in my green VW. Nothing is around. There is only one road. First I see the ocean on the left, and then the ocean on the right. Then there is ocean over the road. I'm not sure whether I should go forward, or turn around and go back. Then I remember feeling: it's a VW. It floats!"

By the end of our time together, Laura's personal confrontation with her psyche had enabled her to develop more of an internal life, an imagination, an aliveness in which she began to trust in her own imagery and the symbols that were emerging in her. Her sliding glass door became a partition that both protected and separated. It represented her ability to keep her ego intact and connected to life. More important, it also represented the beginnings of her ego's constellation to a larger Self.

Laura's growth represents how the psyche begins to serve as a bridge to the Self. Her struggle illustrates a portion of the individuation journey and the workings of the psyche in repairing old wounds and moving us forward.

9

Soul Retrieval: The Lonely One

"We must say "yes" to the spirit even if we do not know it. The spirit in spirit knows us. If we are open to spirit, it pours down on us." (Barry Ulanov, personal communication, June 10, 1999)

CHILD PSYCHOLOGIST D. W. WINNICOTT tells us that in depression and/or creative depression the ego is defending against the death of the false self, or the breakdown of what we experience as our "true self" (Winnicott, 1958;1989). Breakdown is the fear of a past event that has not yet been experienced in the present. Our fear is rooted in an original agony in which our defense system has failed us and our ego-organization has become threatened. Or perhaps, trauma has occurred before there was an ego formed to be threatened. The client, then, might experience the symptoms of depression, but how can it be possible to remember something that has not happened yet, according to the ego? (Madden, 1997, pp. 29–30).

Traces of traumatic severance from one's early caregivers may reside in the unconscious on the level of what Winnicott calls "primitive agony." A person may be plagued by this level of the unconscious since the original experience cannot be gathered up unless the ego can bring the trauma or original breakdown into its present time experience. One remembers, therefore, by experiencing this past trauma in the present for the first time.

In the adult experience of this past event, our maturational experience reverses and we return to an unintegrated state where one might experience absolute dependence upon the analyst-mother to supply enough of an auxiliary ego function to focus upon the sense of emptiness at the core. This emptiness may present itself as deep fear or some form of primitive agony that was associated with the original dependency upon the primary caregiver.

In lieu of absolute dependence upon an analyst, or in the absence of one's analyst, the psyche itself—the underlying presence of the central archetype of the Self (everyone's birthright)—may serve to provide absolute dependence and bridge the fragile ego to the God beyond the psyche for reparation and healing.

Beneath the nothing, we most often locate a something that, when integrated, potentially leads to the development of a more whole self, the self that, through dissociation, trauma, and the wounds we all suffer in infancy, childhood, or even *in utero*, have become split-off fragments of being. The goal here, from a pastoral point of view, is to allow for the emptiness and nothingness, the abyssal chaos, the "divine void" of depression to be witnessed by another or others in order to experience what might have been or what was lost. Discovering the true self, which is creatively alive and real, occurs in the presence of an "other," in relationship.

I am reminded of the biblical New Testament story of Mary Magdalene *waiting*, suffering primordial agony at the empty tomb. The other disciples defended manically to find Jesus and to fix things, and eventually took off. Mary remained at the tomb, in the place of emptiness and silence. Metaphorically speaking, in the context of this discussion, she bent over to look inside the tomb. She confronted the unknown. Eventually someone showed up whom she didn't recognize right away. In truth, a great transformation came about, and it came about in relationship as Mary witnessed the Risen Christ—the first to do so (Ibid., pp. 37–38).

From the above example, I am emphasizing *waiting and silence* as important when we consider the spiritual aspects of depression. We must wait in the silent spaces of isolation, sometimes loneliness, while the psyche prepares us in the place of the unknown for something new. If we have experienced deep hurt, rejection, or injury, we may not feel sure that there is anyone, anything to feel absolutely dependent upon.

Yet, if we can experience the sadness and hopelessness that is buried within us, this kind of suffering helps us to develop a stronger internal reality. When we can tolerate such states, then "taking in" can begin, whether taking in applies to feelings, learning, sex, others, or community. Even if the feeling that emerges is that of a deep wound, at least we are feeling bad about something: at least we begin to feel real.

As we undergo the process of suffering toward the newness and aliveness inherent to working through, or living through, a creative depression, our experience is often close to what many would call religious experience. Having studied such deep encounters in the unconscious with a multitude of patients, John Weir Perry coined the term "spiritual emergency," or acute episode, to describe the distinctness specific to creative depression. He understands the acute episode "not as psychopathology but as an 'altered state of consciousness,' as a 'crisis in growth and development' of such proportions as to throw the psyche into a 'high-arousal state'" (Weir Perry, 1999, pp. 63–64). An acute episode includes:

1. A reordering of the ego, in which we deal mostly with the alienated parts of our egos that begin to undergo a reorganization process.
2. Second, a charged feeling of death and rebirth. We are speaking here of a symbolic death and rebirth—disorganization and reorganization—not about actual death. In the breakdown experience of creative depression, persons most often experience conflicting polarities. Symptoms that flag the proximity of such breakdowns include intense ambivalence, doubt, feelings of alienation, depression, and recurring dreams. These are signs that something unconscious is trying to get our attention, as E. Harding has mentioned, that something is approaching us from within. The activity here is directed by the central core of the psyche, a larger self. From a Jungian point of view, we are speaking of the deepest dimensions of the Self as reflected in the metamorphosis of the person in which the ego is realigned in its relationship to this reality.
3. A third aspect of spiritual emergency is the dominant feeling of regression. Regression restructures the ego by bringing something into conscious awareness that we have to suffer.
4. Fourth, the transcendent function is a crucial factor in the process of healing and integration. The transcendent or religious function is an innate function

of the human psyche that comes about as an intense conflict or wrestling with opposites working toward a synthesizing third resolution of the conflict in the person's psyche. Unfortunately, for many persons suffering from severe depression, the religious or transcendent function is out of reach.

5. Fifth, there is an abundance of imagery. The imagery can be numinous and powerful. This imagery may have to do with an aspect of the god image, regardless of which faith tradition we are speaking.

   Usually, negative aspects of this imagery emerge first, like shadow figures: thieves, devils, ferocious animals, or reptile images. Like inner saboteurs, these inner figures feel as if they are trying to destroy anything positive or life-giving. But we need to hold these internal images in a continuum with other images that eventually arise.

6. Eventually, the person settles into a state of coherency and clarity with a new vision and identity. The ego's experience of dying gives way to "the idea of being born or giving birth. This is the fundamental ground of the whole experience." (Perry and O'Callaghan, 1992, p. 4)

Of the above categories of experience, I would like to say more about the transcendent or religious function. We need to work consciously with the opposites or polarities within our psyches for there to be synthesis and growth of the personality. The transcendent or religious function is an inherent factor in each of us. It functions to mediate the opposite of our experience, and helps us to move beyond one-sidedness or pointless conflict. The transcendent function can facilitate a transition from one psychological attitude to another, and bridge the gulf between the real and the imaginary.

This psychological function is of primary importance for the depressed person since it is often the very function that has been damaged. In the healing process, the focus needs to include this third presence. The transcendent function arises out of extreme conflicts within a person, which the therapist may experience in the transference or countertransference. In the transference, the therapist will carry unconscious aspects of the client and help, over time, to make these conscious to the client. As the tension between the opposites of conflict are held in a dialectical relationship, making room for influences from both sides, eventually the conflict is resolved into a "uniting third," ushering a new synthesis of personality into being.

For the patient, experiencing the transcendent function is always a defeat for the ego since old ways of knowing change. But the suffering is purposive: the defeat of our ego is for our betterment. The symptoms have meaning and *telos*. There is a goal, end point, and specific objective in the process of human development that is unique to each individual in the process of individuation. Individuation may be thought of as an awakening to our own divided nature of unconscious and conscious life and, out of this awareness, the culmination of these elements of our psychological life toward our greatest potential, while recognizing and accepting our human limitations.

In the process of bringing the opposites together in a creative depression, which may include an acute episode or spiritual emergency, some former conflict, some disparity of opposites, is united. We are restored on some level. The transcendent function always makes us new.

How do we recognize the workings of the transcendent function? One of the most obvious ways is when points of view arise in our dreams or waking fantasies that are contrary to whatever position our ego holds. There is a sense of otherness, as if two voices are in dialogue with two contrasting points of view.

We encourage the person in the healing process to reflect about the "otherness" of the contrary viewpoints, image, or feeling, and to place this otherness into dialogue in some form of expression: journaling, art, music, dance, any form that will help to make the polarities of the dialogue more conscious. Yet, most important, the opposites must first be separated before they can begin to integrate.

When the transcendent function fails, it is usually because we either don't have a sturdy enough container to hold the opposites—for example, sufficient ego strength—or the supportive presence of a therapist, teacher, or spiritual director whose ego we can temporarily "borrow from" until our own is more robust. Often, people become impatient and give up too soon.

In relating to the transcendent function, its conscious and unconscious aspects, we are allowing both positions of conflict to become conscious. We allow each position to justify itself, not forcing any resolution. Many contradictions will arise in this imaginal space. By imaginal space, I am emphasizing the difference between fantasy and imagination. Fantasy pertains more to fleeting thoughts of the ego; imagination has to do with the *deeper* flesh of the psyche and carries the greater potential for transformation (Winnicott, 1965 p. 110–11). Winnicott speaks of *deep* as having to do with deep in the patient's unconscious fantasy or psychic reality (by *fantasy,* he is referring to imagination). In our therapeutic work, we are able to use the transference phenomena that relate to the deeper and deeper elements in the emotional development of our patients.

In the transference, he continues, the therapist tries to offer the good-enough mother. The good-enough mother meets the omnipotence of the infant/patient. She does this repeatedly. A True Self begins to have life, through the strength given to the infant's (patient's) weak ego by the mother's (therapist's) implementation of the infant's (patient's) omnipotent expressions (Ibid., p.145). The omnipotent self means allowing for feelings and spontaneous gestures to evolve, that were discouraged, or suppressed, or for which the child was punished.

In the therapy setting, we often experience things that come up in this internal-external dialogue to be divided into opposites such as good and bad, God and the devil, us and them, confusion about moral stance, and so forth. The person may have thought that he or she knew exactly his or her standing in terms of ideologies, morals, the world, and religion. It becomes apparent, during this process, that what we thought we knew has been primarily according to our ego's stance. The opposites in dialogue may suddenly pull us into a new territory where we experience tremendous indecision.

The now-indecisive and floundering ego may become identified with both sides of the opposites, which creates quite a confusion. Splitting, which entails some psychological part of dissociating from consciousness, may arise as a defense mechanism. Beneath the splitting, dissociation, and repression that can accompany creative depression is frequently "a core of madness" that must be uncovered. We feel "mad" owing to the degree of chaos and the loss of equilibrium that our ego is experiencing as its "known" perspectives are challenged.

In this dual identification, it is as if the ego decombusts. Everything is being canceled by its opposite in the dialogue, creating an indecisiveness that is one of the primary symptoms of the depressed condition. In this state of ambivalence, in which everything is canceled out, one may feel like one has fallen into an abyss (Madden, 2003, pp. 117–18).

In this void or abyss, we feel as if we were dying, accompanied by bursts of intense anxiety around conflicting thoughts and values. We feel we have regressed back into the interpersonal field of parents and family. Leftover conflicts arise; for example, whatever was not housed sufficiently by our primary figures in early infancy or childhood.

In the "black hole" of the abyssal experience, conflict can often take on a rather paranoid form (Perry and O'Callaghan, 1992, p. 4). The clash of forces can feel as if one is in an ideological, spiritual, or cultural collision, not just with our former personal ideals and values, but with the entire collective consciousness.

In other words, because dissociation may be occurring on a collective, cultural level, certain individuals may be depressed, not only because of developmental traumatic and intrapsychic factors, but also because of the sensitive and uncanny nature of some individuals to have a large psyche and soul that is more attuned than some of the rest of us to the collective unconscious. This fact underscores the seriousness with which a therapist and client need to be attentive to the individual's dream or waking imagery. Certain persons have access to a depth of unconscious material and, with discernment, may find that their psychic imagery is running parallel to the dissociation or splitting of their culture. Crucially, there is an important cultural factor here. The healing nature of this phenomenon is an ego re-organized in relationship to the Self. Any individual who evolves into a healthy ego-Self relationship inevitably has the potential to contribute a great deal to culture and society. If our society pathologizes such episodes only during which a reordering process is occurring within the individual, we miss the impact of the unconscious material not only upon the individual and his or her growth, but also the potential for this individual's healing to have a positive ripple effect upon the immediate culture and community.

In forging the bridge from creative *de-pression* to creative *ex-pression*, we experience pain. "The soul, as it exits in the territory of its internal cave (when it is seen or dares to be seen), is most often attended by the pain that the healing of splitting brings." (Schwartz-Salant and Stein, 1988, p. 31)

But in the back-and-forth inner dialogue of the breakdown-breakthrough experience of creative depression, even though we may sink into what Winnicott calls "the bottom of the trough," with persistence and faith, we begin to feel the workings of a regulating center. Ann Ulanov takes a turn on the notion of the transcendent function to illustrate for us that there is not only a psychological process at work, but also a transcendent one.

Without intentionally and consciously wrestling with the polarities, or opposites, which are intrinsic to our psychological experience as human beings, the transcendent function remains out of our orbit. Inner conflict and creative depression can actually bring our attention to the deeper layer of our psyche, which is not only purposeful in terms of our healing, but also bears the life-saving potential of soul retrieval. Otherwise, we can end up trapped throughout life, depressed and burdened with contradictory feeling states.

The spiritual emergency or acute episode that J. W. Perry speaks of can last days or weeks, or even years. And yet, as the episode subsides (which one hopes it does, or we may begin to speak of a psychosis), and as the person settles down into a state of coherency and clarity, there may be a feeling of buoyancy, even bliss: feelings of creativity, of fun, playfulness.

If we persist in holding the opposites long enough, allowing the diversity of feelings, thoughts, and projections that we carry to find expression, a new conscious position is born, and born out of the dialogue between conscious and unconscious. This is a symbol. The symbol that unfolds may occur pictorially, in a dream, or in a waking image. Whatever its form, it indicates a synthesis of the opposing elements. The symbol represents a resolution to the conscious conflict.

In sum, in depression, energy (libido, psychic energy) is withdrawn from the external and finds life in the inner world. Depression can facilitate a transformation—a spiritual emergence—by leading us away from the chaotic and unsettling circumference of our lives and toward the center, where we can dig deeply into the unconscious and fully attend to what we discover there. The breakdown-breakthrough experience requires a caring container. It requires empathy and a supportive relationship. It requires release—verbal expression and allowing imagery to pour forth without judging it. The content that emerges needs to be delivered to somebody. The outward movement of communication actually helps to keep the process moving. With proper support and empathy, a person can fall apart and come back together, achieving a major integrative synthesis.

CHRISTINA

I'd like to offer an example of a person in her late twenties who has given me permission, though her name is also changed, to relate her story to illustrate the above. Following an intense period of melancholy brought on by major frustrations in the outside world, she experienced a spiritual and psychological breakthrough of the sort I am speaking of in creative depression.

I worked with Christina for many years. Christina was thirty but with her trim figure and speedy dialogue seemed to be nineteen. Like an excited teenager, she rarely stopped to take a breath, toppling over her own words, rarely making eye contact, looking upward toward the ceiling as she spoke perhaps as a habit developed from projecting out to an audience in her theater work. Although she was personable and engaging in her feisty demeanor, I suspected from the start that her overly confident external self masked tremendous vulnerability and, as I was later to experience with her, profound sadness and hurt that resided in a deeply isolated place.

It was at the beginning of our work that Christina experienced an acute episode accompanied by the shattering in-breaking of numinous experience. We had worked together about three months. I had been doing double sessions with her, and it was her first time in therapy. She was a very passionate person, brimming with a lot of deep feelings, including rage, sadness, and hurt. Before detailing the acute episode, I will give some idea of Christina's life, background, family, development.

Christina was a performing artist. In the recent decade of her life, she had been engaged in an intense period of creative performance, having achieved her goal of performing in a long-running hit musical. Christina had practiced Kundalini in previous years, although she was not practicing currently. She was a person who had engaged with unconscious material by virtue of her artistic and meditative endeavors but without guidance or mentoring.

When she came to me, referred by one of her acting teachers with whom I had worked, her mood had become sullen and inert. Christina had been let go from her idealized show, which she had performed in for five years. Having recently miscarried a baby and, having faced the abandonment of the father of the potential child leaving her after this loss, the director of the show pronounced that she was like "a spring unwound." She told him of her losses, but he was not empathic and was committed only to keeping the show running. Christina felt crushed and betrayed. This director had also taken advantage of her vulnerability as a young and inexperienced actor, and had bullied her in rehearsals threatening her with his critical comments in a way that always succeeding in making her feel that her role was precarious. Behind his sadistic comments was his passive-aggressive punishment for Christina not succumbing to some initial advances he had made toward her once she was cast in the show. His goal was to count her among the many other young women of the cast with whom he had had relations.

Christina had held her ground, taking her role seriously and acting with integrity. But, the director finally pulled a power play over her, catching her off guard, and lied to her about a meeting that he needed to have with her. He had served her alcohol, to which she was somewhat allergic, and she had succumbed to his advances. This fact had made her feel all the worse, soiled, and used, when he announced that he was going to replace her in the show. The trauma of sexual violation also repeated past injuries and traumas.

Being a rather insular person with only a small circle of friends in New York City; Christina had no one to turn to. She had been out-of-town with the show for years and had not had the chance to meet new people. Her fellow actors were competitive and interested primarily in their own successes. Her family lived across the country. All of these factors contributed to strong feelings of isolation, meaninglessness, and ambivalence about her life, her talent, her ability to relate to others.

With this precipitating string of events, her psyche responded to our preliminary therapeutic work with a flurry and outpouring of feeling, mostly the sobbing of deep tears. But she clearly was glad to be connected to someone. She arrived at sessions with a certain bounce of anticipation and even a smile, these emerging from her well-developed actor's persona—one must always "go on." Her bubbly self, however, inevitably melted into sadness by the middle-to-end of each session. Therapy was so new for her. She had never addressed any developmental issues nor worked with her dreams in a reflective way in relation to another person.

A person with an onslaught of feelings like these, which is not to say that she most likely had not been dysthymic throughout her life (dysthymia pertaining to a mood disorder, in contrast to depression, in which low self-esteem, fatigue, poor concentration, hopelessness, and mild eating disorders are typical symptoms), usually has encountered early trauma somewhere between infancy and the age of three. And I would add provocatively that I believe that trauma may occur also in utero, during the time when the infant is still in the archetypal realm of the mother's body the carrier of an a priori knowledge, a preexisting order, an order before the ego comes to consciousness, before being (Jung, 1960, par. 947). As Jungian analyst Erich Neumann states, in the mother's womb, the child possesses (an) absolute knowledge: he or she can see from one end of the world to the other (Neumann, 1989, p. 81). Absolute knowledge activates and directs the archetypal field of the Self "as a deeper regulating and ordering field" (Ibid., pp. 47–49). There is a larger order of being that the mother carries this absolute knowledge of the archetypal realm for the infant in the early stages of its development. If the mother is depressed, or for some reason cannot carry the essence of this archetypal inheritance for the child, the child may be significantly deficient in its ability to connect to Self and soul as it grows and develops.

Christina's father had had a nervous breakdown when she was six months in the mother's womb. We cannot know, but only speculate about the actual effects of an infant's response to the father's breakdown. We do know, from the testimony of one of Christina's aunts, that her mother, although doting upon her newborn, was lonely at the time of Christina's birth and had hoped that having a baby would help her loneliness. There is a good chance that Christina was most likely mirrored by a depressed or minimally dysthymic mother.

Her mother had been wrested from her budding career as a concert pianist to marry when the soldiers came back from World War II. Moving three thousand miles away from her family of origin to the city where her husband had been promised a job, we know that Christina's mother still was overseeing her husband's recuperation at the same time she was nurturing a newborn infant.

The point I am stressing is that even before an infant is born, its archetypal inheritance, its link to the archetypal potential of Self, its birthright of Self-ego evolution, can be disrupted, even severed in utero, and sometimes severely so.

The babe in the womb is in a state of pre-being, a state of somatic oneness with its mother. Initially, it has being only in relation to its mother and is still in a kind of blissful state of union in which it is potentially an ego but not yet. Unitary reality is all that it knows. Ideally, the growing fetus is nestled within that "see-through" place that Neumann speaks of as the original home, a oneness that is present to us through the mother and beyond the mother.

Crucially, the mother is the "window" for this archetypal presence both before birth and after the child is born. She endows the child with this presence like a mirror in her gaze, by the way she touches the child, in how she is able to concentrate upon the child who knows no other Self than the Self of the mother during the early stages of life.

If the infant misses this bridging maternal function, later in life there is something of a synergetic process that draws us into these *Nekyia* episodes. The archetypal presence that is yet unknown pushes through, trying to be known. During these primal, oceanic, contemplative moments of felt union we sense that something knows us. We feel as if there is an objective force or presence that sees us seeing ourselves. And yet, it exists alongside the buried fact of splitting and severance, not only from the mother, but also from an original oneness in which we existed in pre-egoic, pre-differentiated form as a spark about to become incarnate.

Neumann claims that everyone has had prenatal experience of unitary reality (1989, p. 78ff.). We have a blissful state of oneness, but we lose it when we grow into a differentiated ego. We are called back at certain points in our life to this place of unitary reality: in meditative moments, in times of deep prayer, when we regress in therapy or analytic process, at various points of stress and grief, or during creative inspiration.

A depressed mother, without any mental health resources, caring for an emotionally weakened husband and a soon-to-be born child growing within her, plus the stresses of moving and the distance created between herself and her own family most likely contributed to some form of maternal preoccupation, however unintentionally so.

Jung conceptualizes this state of preoccupation as damaging what he calls the spirit link to the somatic unconscious of the still unconscious fetus. Psychoanalyst Wilfred Bion speaks of a mother's preoccupation as the inability of the mother to participate in "reverie," a natural state nearing rapture that occurs during the final two weeks of the maternal gestation period and a few weeks thereafter.

Since the ego hasn't formed yet in utero, if the mother is unable to carry the archetypal bridging function, where does memory get stored if the child is still relying upon its first source?

Jung tells us that memory of our archetypal inheritance is stored in the somatic unconscious—in the bodily unconscious that exists at a very deep level of the psyche. The infant has no ego yet, but when then is the moment of incarnation of the soul? Is it when it becomes incarnate in the flesh? Or is the infant in some way incarnate at its moment of inception?

Traumas and injuries that might occur during the gestation period could not be processed by an infant without the formation of an ego, but the body has its own unconscious. And in utero, it is more complex, because it has its own growing somatic unconscious as well as that aspect of its bodily existence that is still part of its mother's body, the point being that an unborn child certainly could experience trauma while it is in the womb.

The mind-body split in which trauma is buried in the somatic unconscious leaves a person without access to the Self. This somatic dissociation tends to blank out the person's capacity to experience the conflicting opposites. It comes to differentiate feelings from the symptoms our body is expressing. Without the inbreaking experience of breakdown and breakthrough, which stirs the transcendent function into motion, a person can end up trapped throughout life with contradictory feeling states.

Further, I would suggest, following Neumann's notion of "absolute knowledge" and archetypal inheritance, that an infant might also experience, in the birth process itself, some sort of severance from his or her preexistent "heaven," from the world of being, or pre-being that only Being, or the divine Other, knows of.

Jung tells us that pre-egoic trauma is very hard to get to. In most cases with persons who have suffered early trauma one would be working with more emphasis upon the pre-verbal, pre-symbolic world of feelings and trusting that eventually a uniting symbol will arise.

ANOTHER RUPTURE

Christina had further experienced a severe rupture in relationship to her mother when her sister came into the world. Christina was three-and-a-half. Seeing her mother holding the babe in a pale yellow blanket was one of three memories she could recall of her young years. Interestingly, the regressive period during which she experienced breakdown and breakthrough lasted three-and-a-half weeks.

In response to her new sister taking up most of her mother's time, Christina became prematurely independent, spending most of her time outdoors. When she had to be with her mother and sister, her mother put her on a leather "harness" to control her independent spirit. Christina's "omnipotent self," in Winnicott's terms, was surely discouraged and not allowed.

In contrast to her relationship to her mother, Christina's relationship to her father was one of profound idealization. In later years, she was proudly to announce her father's position when asked to do so in school: he was an astro-physicist and the science editor of four encyclopedias who later worked with NASA as Director of Foreign Affairs.

Whereas during her early years, she felt the gleam in her father's eye towards her, over time his increasing workload began to require longer absences. Under greater pressures at work, he became increasingly critical, strict, and irascible as Christina entered junior high school. Her mother, too, gave her very stern parameters and had an extremely critical eye.

By Christina's teen years, her father suffered a partial stroke from stress. Being the parenting child, the child who often ends up looking after her parents' needs even more than her own—often the eldest child—she took on the role of trying to mediate the tension in the family, sometimes having to call the police to stop her father from verbally abusing her mother, a tendency that grew exponentially in a parallel to the nervous tension that her father experienced at work.

Her teen hormones simmering, Christina turned to boys: not so much to replace her father, but to replace the eros of an early maternal relationship, the warm, bodily nurturing, holding, "gleam in her mother's eye," which she had never felt. High-strung with hormones to match, she found a boy a few years older than her in Sunday school, who led her into weekly sexual experiences at the age of thirteen, acts perhaps more aptly described as a rape of her "imperishable personal spirit" (Kalsched, 1996, chapter 1).

Her young body was not prepared for the numerous penetrations by this young man, sometimes up to four at a time. Suffering from an infection, her mother took her to a gynecologist for the first time, and she had to lie about the possible causes of a tipped vagina—something that quite possibly could have influenced her later miscarriage.

She began to feel terribly uncomfortable at church. She had found solace in the church of her early years and had loved to sing in the choir. Now, she was forced to sit between her parents with her mother constantly pulling at her skirt so that the fabric would not ride up above her knee. "Sit up straight like a lady," her mother would whisper during the service.

Christina felt so trapped that she developed a nervous tic, shaking her head back and forth as if trying to shake something off. She began to chew the inside of her mouth until it was raw. Both of these self-destructive gestures made her mother even more furious and punitive.

Her father, an elder of the church, finally pulled the entire family out of the parish because of her behavior. Forbidden to see the young man ever again, she was sent to her room every night after dinner and could not come out until 9 p.m. She was supposed to study during this time, but she could not concentrate and became agitated and restless. She blamed herself for shaming her family but had no one with whom she could talk to about what had happened.

Christina's schoolmates condemned her activity, having filled out through gossip a projection of Christina as "loose" and unworthy of traveling with the popular circles. Christina withdrew to an internalized life, keeping her head turned down toward her books as she walked the halls between classes at school. She felt so alone.

A friend came along, however. Christina hated riding the school bus because boys would scapegoat her by shooting spit wads into her hair. Her new friend Julie, a lovely girl from a warm and loving family, helped Christina to laugh it off, to share stories from the day, and giggle on the ride home ignoring the nasty boys.

Christina's father, unable to direct his angry remarks about the church withdrawal and his own feelings of humiliation displaced them onto Christina's new friend. When Julie would call on the phone, he would mumble in the background: "whore!" She and her father began to fight, using mean language. Christina would become so angry, that she would throw things. Her father would charge up the stairs to thrash her unless she managed to lock the door to her room quickly.

She became celibate for four years. In college, she oscillated between promiscuity and celibacy. By this time, unconscious guilt and shame made the sexual act for her a rather dissociated experience. By the time we began our work together, a few years after she had finished college, performed for five years in her show, and just after her miscarriage, all her hopes and the libido connected to hope for intimacy and relationship had retreated back into her psyche.

Her pain was so deep. She had spent much of her life with a well-established "Self-care" system that actually served as defensive firewalls that were nearly impenetrable. Any form of intimacy, even eye contact, had become difficult for her.

The persecutory part of her psyche was sucking her into a vortex of self-blame: "Am I frigid, sterile sexually" she asked with deep sadness. Certainly, she was not frigid in the physical sense, but the religious or transcendent function was out of her reach.

During Christina's early months of therapy with me, she announced that she was going to undergo cosmetic surgery to change her appearance. The body is so intrinsically connected to the psyche and soul and can feel betrayed when it is cut. It is as if the original wound is amplified. Certainly, her desire to change her appearance was another dissociative attempt to escape from the pain and bodily trauma she had experienced over her lifetime. What I thought Christina's psyche was really seeking (albeit unconsciously), was internal restructuring and renewal, a symbolic, not literal process. The surgery honored her defenses but would not suffice to help her to hold the tension of opposites.

I didn't want to "give her advice" and assume the role of yet another dominating, restrictive parent, but did share my concern about the message she would be giving to her unconscious—that there was something intrinsically wrong with her. She went ahead and had the cosmetic surgery, changing her nose and lifting her face (at the age of thirty.).

THREE-AND-A HALF WEEKS

a human figure held within itself all the loneliness of the world...

Her surgery occurred during my vacation time. During my absence an acute episode began, and Christina fell into a deep regression that lasted three-and-a-half weeks, which spun her into a vortex of abyss. Unconscious material flooded forth.

During the acute phase, the opposites overwhelmed her. In Jung's terms, we slip back into the world of the biological parents but also the primordial and symbolic parents of the archetypal realm. It is not just our developmental injury that exists in the regression, but also the archetypal essence that in some way was not housed sufficiently in early life.

Christina sank into a trancelike state of prayer that lasted for some five hours, curling up into a ball on the floor in tears, blaming herself for all her wrongdoings, especially to her father. Fearing the symptoms she was experiencing, she put in an emergency call to me claiming she thought she was having a nervous breakdown or dying.

"My entire system is shaking. My ego is busting. I'm crumbling apart," she cried anxiously. "I'm cracking out of my skin. Something else is emerging. There's something inside me trembling, dying to come out, to be known, be seen, be loved." Her heartbeat was fast and erratic. She experienced panic anxiety and kept insisting that her death was immanent.

"What specifically precipitated these feelings?" I asked. She explained that she had been terribly upset by a comment that I had made in our last session before my vacation, which she felt too embarrassed at the time to bring up with me. The context of our previous session had been sexuality. She had blamed herself for being frigid and sterile based upon promiscuity. Even women had been sexually attracted to her during her theater years, with whom she had explored kissing and fondling.

Since she had brought it up during the session, I had gently explored the question of her ever having any interest in women sexual partners. My comment apparently set her off. Although she had never been attracted to women, the fact that I brought it up clearly had caused her to ruminate about her other sexual encounters and to doubt her own sexual identify with anxiety, guilt feelings, shame, and deep sadness. She explained that, as a result of her brooding over our conversation about sexuality, she had prayed for some five hours, eventually curling up into a ball on the floor of her apartment sobbing uncontrollably. After so many hours of this cathartic outpouring, she had hit rock bottom and, exhausted, sank into a trancelike state.

"What were you praying about?" I asked.

"Forgiveness for all of my wrongdoings to my father, for being a whore" she replied. Her voice trembled as she spoke.

"What's happening to me?" she asked fearfully.

I explained to her that the wall of defenses that usually surrounded her had fallen down, too much too soon. I reassured her that she was not dying but experiencing huge amounts of anxiety that feel to the ego like it is dying. I suggested that she go easy on the length of time spent in meditative states and call me at any point when it felt to be too much for her, suggesting that she check in with me regularly until I was back in town.

"It might also be helpful to keep a journal," I recommended, "to help contain all the feelings you're having that feel overwhelming. And can you reach out to any of your friends?" I asked.

"I really don't want anyone to know about my surgery," she answered. "Plus, I still have some bandages." I reflected to myself that she had undergone major surgery, with all its incumbent risks, completely by herself.

She took my suggestion of writing in a journal, finding this a natural form of expression. During the three-and-a-half weeks, she completed four notebooks of journaling. She later shared sections of these with me. The dialogue of different internalized aspects of early introjected figures was evident but initially had taken on an almost vehement, particularly negative, threatening, ominous, and daimonic quality.

During the acute phase, one part of her said: "Bust this f— ego. Bust it. I don't want it. Be hard on me. Kill it. The Beast. The Devil. I've killed every relationship that I've ever had with anger and destruction because of this ego and whatever this deep thing is. I want to be a spiritual child, cute, free, soft, and sensual. I'm sick of my gut. Help me. I'm in trouble, Kathryn. All I feel is a gap. Anger and hurt. It's eating me up. Consuming me."

Post-surgery, alone and brooding, the opposites had overwhelmed her. But first, before the opposites differentiated, there was a dominating and overpowering feeling of a dark force that she experienced as annihilating to life. The dominant feeling continued to be of paranoia, fear, and death. The fear would come in waves and threaten to overtake her. "It was like the tremor of an earthquake," she said, "but it was all *inside me*." She called this darker force "the tremendum." It was abyssal.

After she had her last bandages removed and could cover her stitches with her hair, she tried going out to an audition. Uncontrollably, "the tremendum" arose again, and she had to leave the room and go home.

After around a week of this initial abyssal tremor, something shifted. She felt as if some profound presence was entering her body. Whatever this presence was, it was challenging the other, and it felt quite the opposite of "the tremendum." Energy began to surge through her nerve endings and to enliven her as if she were on some potent drug. She was not. In fact, she had never taken any medications and had only mildly experimented with marijuana in her college days.

Holed up in her one-room apartment, alone, brooding and reflective, she knew that some presence was entering her body and psyche and soul, something that she had either never experienced or had experienced and that had been lost.

The opposites polarized to an extreme in her written dialogue. Christina began to write furiously about a conflict between "hedonism and morals." She went back and forth from one side to the other, justifying each position. The shame over her early sexual experience was evident in words of self-hatred and conflict. "I love men, yet I want to destroy their control," she wrote. "Yet, it's so confusing. I also want to be controlled and taken. Do I let the libido live? Is it a demon? I want my lost love, my god, my true inner self and to live in connection with it rather than let things simmer in the deep. I feel as if I am possessed!"

Then the other voice or viewpoint in her psyche would reply: "But sex is not impure. My breasts and body are not impure. Why must I hide them? Why can't I be free? If a person's will is to act outside her mate, is this immoral? I want to hate men for their lust. And yet I have the same lust. So I can't judge—this double standard I impose. I don't need anyone, yet I deeply long for someone. I want total freedom, yet to have total commitment. To come back to the center, but to be free.

"I have equated the devil with sex. In earlier sexual relationships, I just lost myself to what I thought were genuine feelings of passionate love, only to be abandoned, or cheated upon. Abandoned, again, and again. Devil equals man and sex. I need guidance, Kathryn, I need guidance. So many contradictions. What is the truth?"

Within her frenzy of written dialogue, there were signs of a shift. The new feelings aroused and enlivened Christina. She experienced an induced eroticism and began to write about the conflict her psyche was wrestling with as the unconscious material spilled forth. As she responded to the new presence, her writing became spontaneous and automatic.

"It moved my hand," she claimed. "I could hardly stop writing because when I put words on paper, my body shuttered—not with a tremor, but with the most blissful shimmer of feeling I have ever felt. When I'd begin to go to sleep at night, I'd jump out of bed with so many creative thoughts and images that I just had to write them down! This writing never tired me. It made me feel so alive."

In her journaling, there was increasing differentiation as the voices thrashed at each other with their points of view. She held the dialogue open to the more negative and critical voices with an uncanny stamina. This burgeoning ego-strength enabled her previously paranoid feelings of going out in public or seeing friends to subside. The inner shaking and trembling had faded. In its place arose a very unique phenomenon. She described the new experience:

Around two weeks into the three-week episode, a presence entered me with passionate certainty. I was meditating and praying deeply and suddenly felt the urge to penetrate myself with my finger which I had never done before, fearing shame and old memories. What I then felt in my body was like an electrical spasm, a shimmer of energy moving up from the base of my spine all the way up through my third eye.

I ran and grabbed my journal and wrote in large letters, one sentence filling one page: the Coming is at hand. This is it; Christ is a reality! I feel him Coming into me, into consciousness!

A lantern of intense light rose up behind my eyes and illuminated all my thoughts. Literally, I experienced tremendous bright light, and the light was positive, supportive, and good. I seemed to have new knowledge of things I had not known before.

I started reading the Bible daily even though I had not been to a church in seventeen years. Certain words lifted off the page. It was as if these words were holographic, or three-dimensional. They had flesh as well as feeling and meaning and deepened understanding.

When a particular word touched me, my entire body would feel incredible, shimmering electricity, which traveled like a small river within my nerve endings from head to toe. Something I had never known before was present with me, loving me, listening, and responding. This something was very personal and knew me. The more I prayed at night, the more these bodily tributaries shimmered. I felt so loved and so known. I fell asleep with such ease.

I began to discover such new insights, new knowledge, the more I reflected and the more I prayed. This great lantern behind my eyes seemed to inspire new creative ideas that I had never thought of before. I began to design a system of electricity that I intuited exists in the brain pertaining to how thoughts were transmitted. I called a former physician who I had seen while on the road with a theater production and ran my seemingly wild intuitive concepts by him. He actually confirmed some of my thoughts with current brain research being done by a Norwegian scientist.

I realized that I could hold an entirely sensible and intelligent conversation with an educated person and that I was not crazy. I had tapped a new world that resided within me.

Waking up every morning of these weeks became joyous. I felt rested, refreshed, alive with new ideas, and extremely worshipful. Gratitude became all-encompassing. Upon rising, I would begin with a morning ritual, playing music and kneeling with gratitude. The more worshipful I was, the better I felt. Every nerve ending of my body continued to shimmer. I felt the urge to go out and to give to people, to love.

Instead of my former feelings and shyness, even a garbage man on the street passing by became a moment of connection. Instead of averting my eyes, my eyes met his. We smiled. I felt that he was not a stranger, but that we were somehow joined, one, of the same universal reality. I could see a special spark in his eyes that I related to as aliveness and happiness. We acknowledged each other.

The dialogues I had written down during the first week or so became less confrontational and more about coming to understand the deeper meaning and essence of love. The only word I could come up with to express what I was feeling was bliss. I felt little hunger for food and had little impetus to eat. I did eat, but it wasn't motivated by need or anxiety. All that I had ever wanted and had ever longed for was in this presence that was living in me, through me. During those three-and-a-half weeks, this incredible presence illuminated my soul.

Heart Flower

Imagery began to tumble across my awareness, images that arose on their own. I didn't have them "in mind;" they just emerged. I had a tremendous urge to express myself in pictures. I sketched myself holding a lotus flower in full bloom that was emerging from my heart. A mandorla, or oval shape of flames, surrounded my body as if I were being purged by fire. I think that this picture shows the demonic side of hedonism in the flames, but I am being freed. Within the flames, I am smiling. I entitled the picture *Heart Flower*.

The next picture was of a giant multi-petaled flower, each petal bursting forth with thousands of tiny seeds. The flower was a magnified version of the flower or the heart in my first drawing.

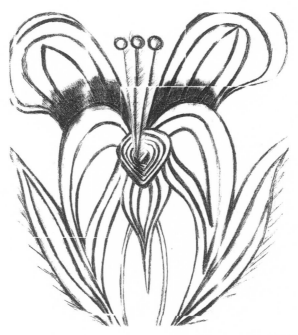

Feeling freed, Christina continued to unfold like a multi-petaled blossom, replete with self-fertilizing properties fueled by her budding relationship to the never-ending fecundity of the unconscious.

The flower seemed to be lotus-like and of mythological dimensions. On an archetypal level (Cooper, 1987, pp.101–2), J. C. Cooper describes the lotus as a universal symbol, a symbol of mythological dimensions. It is considered by some cultures to represent indefinite possibilities, creation, renewal and immortality. The Taoist tradition views the lotus as The Golden Flower, which is a symbol of spiritual unfolding and the heart.

The lotus is particularly associated with the Great Mother as a lunar goddess. In association with this archetype, it represents the formation of the receptive feminine principle. At the same time, it emphasizes both the life-giving and death-dealing powers of the Great Mother. As with any archetype, we find the duality of manifestation, and the tension of the opposites as the process of transformation and individuation unfolds into ultimate unity.

The process of individuation depicted by the lotus portends to a spiritual unfolding as it grows upward through the waters, and flowers in the sunlight. Its seed pods are the fecundity of creation. In bud form, it represents all potentiality; in bloom it depicts expansion, enlightenment; the heart; divine birth.

In Buddhist culture, the lotus of the heart is solar fire; the unseen and all-devouring; the unfolding of all existence; peace; harmony; union. Analogous to the lantern Christina beheld behind the eyes of her mind, the Buddhist symbol emphasizes the notion of an illuminating wisdom that relies upon the spiritual flowering of the lotus.

In the Chinese tradition, the lotus represents purity, spiritual grace, peace, and feminine genius. In the Hindu tradition, the lotus represents the highest culmination of consciousness and wholeness. The lotus is the self-generative; the self-born, the immortal and spiritual nature of humankind; the unfolding of all possibilities: eternal regeneration, superhuman origin, and beauty.

Christina sketched a third, forth, and fifth drawing. The last picture in the series was a depiction of a giant Iris expressing with a bold passion three stamen thrusting forth out of a darkened center. Christina called the stamen "the trinity," since "they emerged from a center that was infinite."

She wrote a few days later, "In my meditation, Ira (her current boyfriend) flashed—then my father—then Christ. My arms filled with energy and a soulful, joyous feeling.

This intuitive and felt bodily knowledge—literally felt, but symbolically meaningful—continued to pour forth with the same spontaneity as had her automatic writing. Completely in contrast to the process of rational or discursive thought, Christina *knew* that Christ was real, that he was coming, and that this knowing was inspired from a passionate new reality that surged into her consciousness, especially inclusive of her body.

Daily tasks became joyful. She filled up a bucket of water and used wood soap to scrub every inch of her apartment floor on her knees. Scrubbing the floor became an "act of love." She knew no other way of describing it. "What I normally would have considered to be work became a loving offering," she claimed. "It was as if I was doing the scrubbing in relationship to someone and out of love."

In the back and forth of Christina's inner dialogue, she began to feel the workings of a regulating center. Something very tangible and real responded to her as her ego dissolved to make way for the symbol. Emerging from the viewpoints of the opposites flowed a deep, embodied feeling of love: love for herself, renewed love for others, and hope.

"All these years I've been so confused. Men are not the devil," she said. "There can be love in the body. Sex is not sin or whoring. Sex can be something to give. We can *become* the love."

The opposites were uniting into a synthesizing third, a unity. Even though her written imagery was of Christ, a male, the recovered sense of spirit in her body, the *jouissance*, the reverie, the experience of spirit in the body was distinctly in the realm of the archetypal feminine spirit, a union so lost or unavailable to her from her early life. Without the experience of union, no incarnation (Schwartz-Salant and Stein, 1988, p. 32).

As she described the latter part of the three-and-a-half weeks, which had now transformed her every day into simple, joyful living, she said that she met with friends in the park and went to the beach. They would engage in long and intimate conversations during which they unanimously commented upon the clarity of her thought processes. Her friends commented that they had never experienced her as being so lucid. It was as if a new intuition resided in her—a grounded knowing.

Toward the end of these weeks, however, something changed. Christiana was so elated with this new exuberance of daily living life that she spoke to people about it more and more. She found that people were drawn to her and wanted to stay around her. Yet, something was slipping away. Her rational mind began to intrude upon the wonder of this feeling of primary unity and this nurturing archetypal presence.

As she felt some of the shimmer in her nerve endings diminish, she tried to hold onto the feeling with the conscious grasp of her mind. The more her ego-mind penetrated the experience, the more it began to fade. She began to fear losing this wondrous gift that had felt like a descent from heaven and prayed every morning and evening to be able to remain in this state of being.

But decreasing in intensity every day, at the end of three-and-a-half weeks, the illuminative lanterns behind her eyes were now gone. She transitioned back into her normal ego state. However, she comprehended a new wisdom that was to remain with her as a turning point. Through experience, she believed the unconscious to be an absolute reality that had endowed her with a wiser, more humble, more relational, more hopeful personal identity. She did not grieve the loss of this immediate profoundly loving "other." Instead, with some hesitation, she sought out a few churches in the city.

One morning, she looked through the yellow pages, chose a church location, and got herself ready to go to a service. She was totally surprised to find herself sitting on a pew next to another young woman from her home town—of all the churches in New York City—and on this particular day of "coming out" of her three-and-a-half-week journey.

From this point on, the three-and-a-half weeks would always mark for her the experience that transformed her life, an episode that convinced her that a divine feminine presence was actively available to her, that she was distinctly known and received by this presence, and that this spirit was with her in soul and body.

As cited earlier, Jung has expressed this space of healing in the beautiful expression that "we count for something only because of the essential we embody" (Jung, 1963, p. 325). In Christina's journey, I clearly observed a link to the infinite and the beginnings of an awareness of her own unique "essential." Her form of *Nekyia* had been purposive as a necessary step in connecting with an embodied sense of the infinite.

In a creative depression, then, psychic energy is withdrawn from the external and finds life in the inner world, which can facilitate a transformation through engagement with the transcendent function—a spiritual renewal—by leading us away from the chaotic and unsettling circumference of our external lives and toward the center of our true selves.

The symbolic death that I have been speaking of is like being on a cross gazing into the void, or staring into the empty tomb. It feels very lonely. It may feel like a black hole or antimatter because what we are confronting is what is truly *un-conscious*, unknown.

But I am suggesting that it may be required of us—at one point or another—to suffer the symbolic death that accompanies a conscious reconciliation of the opposites so that something new comes into being that has the effect of continuously incarnating the God image. In light of this notion, the depressed may certainly be symptom bearers of a *dis-eased* society, while bearing the possibility of an immensely spiritual path that includes healing potential for the collective culture.

Truly the words of Francis Wickes, cited earlier (1950, p. 245), express the profound unity of the meeting of human and the divine. Her words express the stunningly beautiful image of hope. We might think of this journey as encountering "the dark light of the soul:"

> the One hung and gazed down into the void...drawing all solitude unto itself...deep in the fathomless dark was born an infinitesimal spark. Slowly it rose from the bottomless depth, and as it rose it grew until it became a star. And the star hung in space

just opposite the figure, and the white light streamed upon the Lonely One.

In our creative response to creative depression, I would hope that we might know and experience such "light dawning behind the darkness."

THROUGH THE AIR HOLE

"This journey toward home begins, and can begin, only at the abyss, at that place where all the props of ego consciousness have fallen away and we stand naked and alone in an alien world under a darkened, winter sky." (ROMANYSHYN, 2000, P. 195)

To WHERE HAVE we come at the culmination of this brief journey? It is my sincere hope that together we have reached a common ground of understanding that the experience of the abyss or the Pleroma is more than one that merely frightens with its glimpses of radical otherness. I would hope we could agree that it is also one that is plump with meaning, the experience of which may lead to reunion, integration, and individuation.

I have found myself wondering if we are not, perhaps, touching on the mystery of our origins in these explorations, and that this is why we feel the touching both at such a profound depth and with such ambivalence. I mentioned earlier that in traditional Christian literature the abyss has often been likened to the sea, referencing St. Hilary of Potiers, who says, "The sea is the gloomy abyss" (Jung, 1989, par. 255). From our physical origin on this earth, the sea produces a twofold response in us. We are drawn to it because we find it beautiful and alluring. It is our original home. But we are also repelled by it and fear it because of its unknown depths. It has become foreign geography to us. We fear we cannot breathe there. The sea is the perfect representation and icon of the physical abyss.

In much the same manner, the *Ungrund*/Pleroma draws us in: it is our spiritual origin. Yet, it also repels us because of a similar fear of its unknown depths. It is foreign to our sense of ego/self, and yet it may offer the experience of unitary reality that brings about a new alignment of ego-Self, in which we find both our illumination and our individuation. Boehme's vision of the *Ungrund* and Jung's of the Pleroma are perfect symbols of this spiritual abyss.

Jungian analyst Robert Romanyshyn explores a vision of the abyss as a place where we stand with our grief over loss, but where we are also met with something else, something that is unexpected. First, he says, "we are drawn to the abyss when we no longer experience the presence of the Divine in the world" (Romanyshyn, 2000, p. 197). But we meet something else there, something that is shared by Boehme in his vision of light on a pewter dish, by Jung in his *Nekyia*, by Laura in her mandala dream of wholeness, and ultimately by Christina in her symbol of the lotus. That something is beauty.

> It is a wonder to me that it is at the abyss that we meet Beauty, at the turning points of the soul, in the depths of passion, suffering and sorrow. (Ibid., p. 200)

Above all, I have tried to offer some reflection and examples pertaining to the "turning points of the soul," and the deep experience of unitary reality that is to be found there. For Jung, this reality is one that reveals the Self, the archetype that unites all opposites, and one that is "open at both ends." On the near end, it is open to our earthly life of the ego. On the far end, it is open to the divine. We see through this passage to the Self-revealing reality, a reality that is shown in the experiences presented here to be one which is also continuously coming toward us. It gives life by penetrating and uniting the human being to layers of existence in and through the human psyche.

Boehme wove these experiences into a complex theosophical system that admits of a direct apprehension of God. Through an integration of Christian theology and alchemical symbolism, Boehme has left behind for us a map for the soul's journey to God, and has offered us a connection between the inner and the outer worlds, saying in *The Way to Christ* that the "inner ground...will also...rule over the external rational life of the stars and elements" (1915, p. 210). In other words, the inner and hidden governs the outer and apparent. In *Mysterium Magnum*, Boehme speaks of yet another opposition of inner and outer, above and below:

> The angelical world is called *above*, and the formed outward is called *below;* in manner as we may say when a fire is enkindled, then the light is above, and the substance (or matter) below. When we speak of God's (being) *above*, then we mean and understand *within*, for the (being) within, without the substance, is the (being) above; for without the substance (or matter) there is all above, no below; that which is under the substance is also above. (1965, p. 396)

It has never been my intention here to delve into scholastic speculation as to the exact "spiritual coordinates" of the abyss. Just this: I believe Boehme has given us an important clue in the above passage. The abyss is both beyond and *within*, which for Boehme also means above or transcendent. It is the place of intersection of the human spirit with the divine. The place where we look through the "window on eternity," from the human to the divine and back again.

In a provocative piece entitled "The Self and Not-Self in Christian Mysticism," Ewert Cousins contrasts images of affirmation in St. Augustine and negation in Meister Eckhart. He describes St Augustine's direct experience of God as occurring in his "inmost part" (*in intima mea*).

> We can say that Augustine experienced an immediate contact with the divine as eternity, truth, and goodness (love). This encounter took place in the depths of his soul, in the innermost recesses of his consciousness (*in intima mea*). (Cousins, 1990, p. 64)

While there are more corollaries to be drawn between Eckhart and Boehme in their pushing beyond positive imagery of God into the realm of the imageless abyss, I would like to draw a connection between Augustine and Boehme and Jung on two points: one, each claimed *direct experience of God* and two, each spoke of the mirror or the *speculum*.

Not all of those who do theology can make a claim of direct experience of God. Cousins tells us this experience occurred for Augustine *in intima mea;* Boehme would have found this phrase a fitting description of the inner journey. Cousins is careful to point out that Augustine is not talking about a *disappearance* of the soul or the self. Neither is Boehme or Jung, and neither am I. Although we have seen that a diminution of the ego is often a precursor to the experience of unitary reality, we do not disappear. We do not merge as a drop of water into the sea. We have identity, we are known, and we know that we are known. Augustine discovers on the inner journey,

> into the depths of himself that he himself is an image, or, as the medieval tradition emphasized, a mirror (*speculum*) of God. Thus the self retains its own intrinsic constitution ontologically, theologically and mystically. However, it does not stand in radical isolation; on the contrary, in its very ontological and spiritual depths it is relational. (Ibid., p. 64)

On the other hand, recalling the distinction Cousins makes between *kataphatic* and *apophatic* experience, I would argue that at the depth of re-membering in the dark abyss of the *Ungrund*/Pleroma experience, it is a matter of both/and. I believe that the Self does touch the ontologically divine beyond the positive attributes of the Trinity, however momentarily. The soul is undifferentiated but remains in image. The contents of this experience are brought back to consciousness including the contents of the nothingness itself. It is as if the apophatic makes the kataphatic possible. One form of experience houses and fulfills the other. Each relies upon the other for a complete *coincidentia oppositorum* (Cousins, 1992, pp. 93–95).

The mirroring is the activity that is especially mutative in the "bringing back" and integrating into life. As Augustine likens the soul to the *speculum* or mirror of God, we find a plethora of mirror imagery appearing in the works of Boehme, some of which I have previously referenced; for instance, Antoine Faivre with respect to the importance of the mirror for Boehme, relating it to Boehme's description of the "first event," the creation of the Divine Wisdom, Sophia.

In his *Six Theosophical Points* Boehme, himself, says,

[W]e recognize the eternal Un-ground out of Nature to be like a mirror. For it is like an eye which sees, and yet conducts nothing in the seeing wherewith it sees. (1958, p. 6)

And then the mirror of the eye, viz., the Father's and Son's wisdom, becomes manifest, and wisdom stands accordingly before the Spirit of God, who in it manifests the un-ground. (Ibid., p. 9)

Not only is Sophia, the eternal eye, the first event and opposition so that God could have self-understanding, Boehme also appears to regard Sophia as a fourth to the Trinity (Ibid., pp. 8–9). Boehme's recognition of the place of Sophia in the godhead—fully three-hundred years before Jung acknowledged the Roman Catholic Church for the watershed doctrine of the Assumption of the Virgin Mary—happened at the very time when the feminine was being cast out of a good portion of mainstream Christianity with the coming of puritan Protestantism.

Jung, too, acknowledges Boehme's Sophianic mirror, describing it as "a summa of secret knowledge (Jung, 1967, par. 31). Both Boehme and Jung are dealing with a bridge to the Absolute through which they get a glimpse of something beyond the psyche. I have already pointed out the similarities in the nature of that experience and the basic map that each offers as helpful to clinical suffering. From Boehme's point of view, Sophia gives us a model for the eternal couple. The *coniunctio* (*hieros gamos*) is a universal one in heaven, already contained in the *Ungrund*. The efficacy of the preexistent Sophia/Wisdom in Boehme's schema is that she both gives birth to and is wedded to Christ. But is Christ (who does "cross over") the only bridge to Sophia (who does not)? Can we know Christ without the medium of the psyche and the Self?

Although I do not intend to compare or contrast Christ with the Self here, certainly some provocative questions come to mind in the context of what difference it makes in our conceptualization and experience whether Christ or the Self is our model of the eternal couple and what exactly they might have to do with each other remembering that, according to Jung and Neumann, the Self is a preexistent potentiality for all; but not all faiths have Christ as their guide and redemptor.

Since my focus is primarily clinical, the question I would raise is: What difference does it make clinically that the contraries coexist eternally, as in the Pleroma/*Ungrund* level of spirit? Sophia as a mirroring reality of the eternal couple and her analogous function to that of the Self might pertain to what the Self symbol looks like clinically in the reality of the field created between the two people in the room that focuses upon the patient's reality and images of the Self. This would imply that the archetypal is a layer of being, an air hole to a before-being; a larger, unitary reality that we all participate in and can know about.

I am talking about an experience "in the body" in which spirit conjoins with matter in such a way that we know this original unity, this original predifferentiated conjunction. Neumann's developmental schema takes us back to prenatal, and I am taking us back one step more.

Perhaps there is an experience of an eternal *coniunctio* that must happen in the Self-body-field of the analytic couple as spirit in the body, spirit in chthonic matter that redeems the body to the level of the Pleromatic couple. Perhaps it takes a suffering breakdown to remember the original nature of being and what is and was actual. The point is that something breaks through and addresses the patient's suffering in a profound way in which the person feels held and known and distinct and real. In some way, the person is able to make meaning out of his or her experience where there was none before.

This, I believe, is what Boehme means by "spirit" in his phrase, "and then the Spirit did break through" (1915, p. 487). Whereas Jung never completely defined Pleroma, from a metaphysical standpoint he knew it. He had experienced it and witnessed its reality. Based upon his Pleroma experience, he proceeded to search for a concept that would fit what he had known as a conjunction of spirit and matter, and found that the Self field must intersect what he called the *unus mundus* level of *coniunctio* to replicate this level of experience or seeing through.

CONIUNCTIO WITH THE UNUS MUNDUS

The unitary experience is a union of opposites in which a particular image appears followed by a flooding of images that first combine the opposites in a harmonious field and then divide them into pairs that keep unfolding. In the dividing we see unfolded the future of the Self, a signaling of the beginning, both for Boehme and Jung, as well as the end that is to become, finally, the *mysterium*. (It is interesting to note that Boehme's last major work was the *Mysterium Magnum*. Jung's ultimate contribution to his collected works was entitled *Mysterium Coniunctionis*.)

In speaking of the contents of the collective unconscious, Jung says that the "indistinguishableness of its contents gives one the impression that everything is connected
to everything else" and "despite their multifarious modes of
manifestation, they are at bottom a unity" (1989, par. 660).
I believe that Jung's six years of *Nekyia* led him definitively
to his vision of a unitary world, the *unus mundus* being for
him an image of how we engage, at the psychoid layer of the
unconscious, in a particular kind of seeing through to layer
beyond layer of existence, each layer intimately connected
with all other layers.

I have identified the psychoid, archetypal layer of the
collective unconscious as a deep layer of existence in which
a breakthrough experience of the numinous points to a pre-
differentiated reality, a universal conjunction that is a state
of original unity from which we emerge. We are created in
this image, and we return to this original ground, distinct
and known.

Of course, there is not really any way we can claim the
fact of a preexistent, predifferentiated ground or prove preexistence as an original unitive ground, or un-ground. How
can anyone claim that he or she is created in the image,
or any image, of something that wills us into existence in
conjunction with love? How can parents know what their
children will be like until they have incarnated and are free
to establish wills of their own? At some point, will that
new seed of being dig down so deep into the soil of where it
came from (beyond DNA) and connect in a meaningful way
with a preexisting oneness?

My only claim to this possibility is based upon the
fact of Boehme and Jung's experience, from studying the

testimony of many who have recorded their experiences, from what I have experienced personally and through years of working with patients and students.

Boehme and Jung experienced a predifferentiated unitary reality during those years preceding their writing about it and spent the rest of their lives trying to sustain, express, and make sense of what it was that they had experienced. Both set about to develop a map of it that is useful to others.

As I have already illustrated, central to Jung's map are the notions of Self and Self-field. Another concept that he developed in the context of the Pleroma experience was that of the *coniunctio oppositorum*, an alchemical term meaning a union of opposites that occurs between unlike substances. Certainly Jung had experienced firsthand various levels of *coniunctio* during the period of his inner journey, and was still refining these concepts forty years later in his writing of *Mysterium Coniunctionis*.

To help illustrate the three stages of *coniunctio*, Jung drew primarily from Gerard Dorn, a medieval alchemist. I have already described the first stage, *unio mentalis*, in the context of a patient example. The second step reunites the liberated spirit with matter in a new and higher synthesis. Jung writes that at this second stage of conjunction the individual has grasped a certain "knowledge of his paradoxical wholeness" (Brome, 1981, p. 241). Based upon what I have said about the Self-field, a person at this stage has probably encountered breakdown or *breakthrough* to unitary reality at a level sufficient to constellate the Self. The question is now whether or not the person will continue to receive what is ongoing and manifest in relation to the unconscious, and to allow the radical otherness of spirit to transform his or her way of being and knowing.

The third and most important stage of conjunction is the transforming union with the *unus mundus*, the one or *unitary world*. In *Mysterium Coniunctionis*, Jung references Dorn's description of the *unus mundus*, saying that it,

> affords us a deep insight into the alchemical *mysterium coniunctionis*. If this is nothing less than a restoration of the original state of the cosmos and the divine unconscious of the world, we can understand the extraordinary fascination emanating from this mystery. (1989, par. 662)

It is as if Jung is suggesting a reunion of the individual soul with the timeless flux of the beginnings of creation. As Jung writes, "the third and highest degree of conjunction was the union of the whole man with the *unus mundus*." This *unus mundus* is for Dorn (and Jung) "the eternal Ground of all empirical being, just as the self is the ground and origin of the individual." Jung goes on to say that this third degree of conjunction is universal and signifies "the relation or identity of the personal with the supra-personal" (Ibid., par. 760ff).

The union of the individual with the *unus mundus* in the mind of God is a reunion of the original nondifferentiated unity of the world, or Being, with us, who are a part of the multiplicity (von Franz, 1975, p. 248). In fact, this *coniunctio* puts us squarely in both worlds—the multifarious world of the opposites, which we inhabit in our ego consciousness, and the *unus mundus*, the one world beyond all opposites in which all is conjoined. We then become as amphibians, inhabiting two worlds: one foot in heaven and one on earth.

Dorn describes the experience of the *unus mundus* as the opening of a "window of eternity" (or "air hole") into the eternal world. In fact an experience of the Self helps us to extricate ourselves from the stifling prison of a conscious image of the world that is too narrow, so that we can be open to the transcendent that can touch and move us. Our finite life has meaning only when it is related to the infinite through the "window on eternity" (von Franz, 1975, p. 250).

Jung touches upon this in *Memories, Dreams and Reflections*, when he says,

> The greatest limitation for man is the "self"; it is manifested in the experience: "I *am only* that!" Only consciousness of our narrow confinement in the self forms the link to the limitlessness of the unconscious. In such awareness we experience ourselves concurrently as limited and eternal, as both the one and the other. (1963, p. 325)

Thus, the experience of the connection of our personal self to the archetypal Self is a concentration of one's being into the particular and, at the same time, the "boundless enlargement" of the Self, both as center and circumference (von Franz, 1975, p. 251). William Blake's words come crisply to mind: "To see a World in a Grain of Sand...and Eternity in an hour" (Blake, 1988, p. 147).

Along with Boehme and Jung, we emerge from the experience of unitary reality with inner knowledge, with an awareness of our connectedness to the *unus mundus*. Yet, we cannot live continuously in the image of the abyss or the Pleroma, just as we cannot live long in any mystic vision. We can relate, however, "through the air hole" to our abyssal or pleromatic experiences.

It is important to note that in the case of Boehme and Jung, as with many others, the initial experience of unitary reality itself comes at the beginning of the individuation process, not its culmination. Jung believes it to be,

> significant for the whole of alchemy that in Dorn's view a mental union was not the culminating point but merely the first stage of the procedure. The second stage is reached when the mental union, that is, the unity of spirit and soul, is conjoined with the body. But a consummation of the *mysterium coniunctionis* can be expected only when the unity of spirit, soul, and body is made one with the original *unus mundus*. This third stage of the *coniunctio* was depicted after the manner of an Assumption and Coronation of Mary, in which the Mother of God represents the body. (1989, pars. 664–66)

What I have been describing, this process of conjoining culminating in the third *coniunctio*, has to do with incarnation and enfleshment. It is the rejoining of spirit and matter to the original unity, in order to become spirit-in-matter. Psychologically, we may think of this process as the reclaiming of the split-off parts of the disjointed person on the road to individuation. For Boehme, this process is represented by his placing of Sophia as the preexistent fourth to the Trinity in the Godhead.

SPIRIT AND REALITY

Why do we call what we see in analysis a *coniunctio* and leave it at that? What if the *coniunctio* were a memory? Perhaps what we are experiencing in these glimpses of unitary reality is an ancient memory of when the opposites were together.

When we have "seen-through" to the radically other otherness of spirit breaking in, the tendency is perhaps to try and continue to sustain the relationship of spirit-in-matter as a focus of utmost value and worth. Knowing about this event in our experience requires *re-membering* it again and again, as I have illustrated clinically, and with Boehme and Jung. Re-membering is an endeavor that takes place "in the body," that involves others, and for which depth psychology becomes one container, and contemplation, as with Boehme, another. The centrality of a spirit-in-matter focus adds something specific to the intersubjectivity of the analytic setting. It adds the *vas*, the vessel, the body that spirit can potentially penetrate in terms of the analytic relationship, offering a new layer of otherness at a deeper depth, with a fuller dimension.

But, as with most things that occur in the body, neither of these endeavors is without suffering. As the patient suffers the discomfort of opposites, "personal development" eventually thrusts up against the "integrating and individuating self" (Horne, 1998, p. 23). At this juncture, if analyst and patient are willing to encounter and to engage the unfamiliar in the primary process of the unconscious beyond the level of projective identification, beyond what Ricœur refers to as secondary, derived, or objectified forms of illusion, the patient may shift toward a sphere of inner existence rooted in an active, dynamic, and generative flow of being. In one male patient's experience after three years of analytical work, this shift has been described as a radical uprooting from "an imperative mode of doing to an indicative mode of being," an ongoing and lived experience that makes him feel "transported, carried along by the personal and the transpersonal" (personal communication, with permission from the patient, 1999).

Instead of feeling "driven and squeezed," as he had his whole life, defended against the woundedness and vulnerability of being alone, even though he still felt "wobbly and uncertain," he also experienced a "calm, stability and solidarity."

> I feel like I am receiving the space I was never allowed to have or was not deserving of. And the mystery of the space is awesome. It just dawned on me, the extravagance of this space. I'd like to give others this space because I know what it's meant to me—this extravagance. It's like the difference between abundance and depletion, and I choose abundance, life.
>
> D. expressed this flow of being further within the context of his Christian faith.
>
> And what Jesus is asking us is to engage the fullness of life with the fullness of ourselves. What really matters is that we are in touch with the ground and source of our life, and that we live as fully into that as we are given the grace to do. That in true surrender comes a fullness and abundance and love we could never have imagined before. That in the giving of ourselves...we find the way of life, of all the promises of Christ that transcend this life, whatever befalls us. We can race furiously until we are raced out and can race no more. Or we can try a different tack. We can realize that our hearts are as important as our heads....Maybe more so. Jesus asks, after all, not for our heads, but for our hearts. He wants our center, not what's left over. But if he *has* our center, there is more left over than we could ever have imagined. (personal communication, 1999)

In this sense, the Self is both center and circumference, both personal and social. We become a person in relation to others, engaged in an *act* where spirit moves freely (Berdyaev, 1946, p. 56). This act may become a center from which all else in life flows, actualizing values and community. Jung envisions community as an ever-widening circumference that emerges from an authentic and generative sense of Self that recognizes the value of every person.

Depth psychology, as it participates in a conjunction of transcendent spirit with personal spirit, can lead beyond our being a fragmented part to our becoming a particular part of a larger whole. Our psychological process, developmental and symbolic, can be measured in history, in the concrete world of bodies where community becomes an extension of oneself, the body incarnate.

Spirit is an *actuality*, and desire is a crucial tool in the experience of unitary reality. Desire can be understood as an intense longing, a yearning to conjoin with spirit and to incarnate. Human nature passionately seeks unitary reality and something responds, seeking us—deep calls unto deep. The back and forth I have described in the previous case example builds a relationship of mutuality, inner and outer, and we are spiraled forward in a process of becoming.

The issue becomes less, "How do we rid ourselves of desire so that we can merge with this larger self?" and more, "How do we receive a Self so large and maintain personal identity without losing the ego?"

If we choose to maintain personal identity, then the soul, the heart or essence of the person endowed with the potential for conscious relationship to Deity (Jung, 1968, pars. 9, 10, 11), becomes the province of depth psychology, and we engage in a method that involves a sensing of the soul's presence through the symbol and its archetypal

source. Without the soul, and the space of facilitating conditions to experience the soul as passionately compelling
the total personality, we miss the flesh of a truly symbolic
life where symbols arise in the immediacy of religious experience experienced in and through the psyche, and we miss
the vital encounter of the *reality* of spirit, the essence of a
transubjective other, which is what endows the soul with a
personal identity that is continuous.

Underlying our ability to receive is the basic premise that
we receive because we are received. As receivers and heal-
ers, we are at our best when we are celebrating and receiving what is there just before us. Receptivity conjoined with
passion leads to our urgently offering everything over to
consciousness, to corresponding with what is already there
and receiving us. Ultimately,

> we go beyond the ego, and in a sense, we must keep
> returning—with the attention—a going in from the
> outside. We become one with objects, unite with them,
> with part of the world. Uniting is sort of a multiple
> mirroring—a *sensus communis* in which our sense
> of objects is reflected in us and us in the objects. The
> objects in some way respond to us. It feels as if some-
> one is looking in the mirror at us looking at ourselves
> in the mirror. The world becomes entirely present; it
> has presence. (Madden, 2001, p. 198–199)

It is "a triumph with and through the concrete, over
the concrete" (Ulanov, B. 1973, p. 419). In such correspondence, we equip ourselves for levels of personal communion
that truly surprise us.

SPIRIT OF THE FIRE-FLASH

In *The Passionate God*, theologian Rosemary Haughton speaks of passion and personal communion in simple terms. In the loving exchange between two persons, love is given and received. Received, it is returned in response, equaling an exchange (Haughton, 1981, pp. 18–46).

What becomes evident and necessary for passionate love to break through is the prerequisite of a weak spot, a vulnerability in us. Something happens that shakes us loose from our moorings of settled attitudes and creates a response that transforms what was vague longing into intense passion. Passion is a dynamism that is unmistakably more than a "drive toward, or desire for." We feel it in the body, but it is not mere instinct. As we are shaken from our known moorings, we experience a radically other otherness so profound as to be ineffable. Thus, the experience is often described as an abyss, or a void. We do not need knowledge, at this juncture, only willingness to receive the thrust that penetrates the gap of unknowing.

If we can hold ourselves open to receive, this passionate otherness may become so concentrated at the point where it strains against unknowing that it breaks through as an impulse that overcomes our defended barriers and passes us through to a new and desired sphere of experience (Haughton 1981, pp. 58–61). This is not the kind of love that depends upon the existence of its object as lovable. Haughton understands passionate love as desire opening "at both ends."

Most often, human nature deflects experience at the level of passionate love, Haughton says, because it is too much of a struggle to differentiate. We have to be able to receive the passionate thrust of otherness and to allow our desire to mobilize.

Jung understands desire as reflecting intentionality in the phenomenological sense. The reductive intends the prospective, and vice versa, so we can go back into history, into the primal, unconscious, and forward into possibility. Thus, we find an intentionality of desire where desire encounters and embraces other desire, even an opposite or opposed desire. If anything, desire gets bigger because it comes into a fuller reality as it meets its opposite, and the more we grow interiorly, the more we can hold.

When the *reality* of spirit hits us, everything begins to become more clear to us. Decisions we have to make begin to relinquish their driven quality of anxiety, and our other frivolities begin to fade. As Barry Ulanov once said to me, "our fat-headedness and fussing become more amusing than persecutory as we stop hiding from consciousness and put a halt to everything that numbs it." We no longer care (as much) whether we are at the top of the heap reaping honors. The lure of arguing endlessly over hegemonies, ideologies, and quick fixes fades, as we begin to give up our human tendency toward surface immediacy.

We find that, by placing what is important first in the order of being, everything comes that is important. All other things begin to pass—not in the sense of a quietism, but as a lived reality of embodied passion and compassion where what evolves is continuously and dynamically new.

All Is Together an Eternal Magia

There was a Birth, certainly,
We had evidence and no doubt, I had seen birth and
  death,
But had thought they were different; this Birth was
Hard and bitter agony for us, like Death, our death,
We returned to our places, these Kingdoms,
But no longer at ease here, in the old dispensation,
With an alien people clutching their gods.
(Eliot, 1962, p. 70)

In *Six Theosophic Points*, Boehme reveals what appears to be the very key to his understanding of God's relationship to Himself and to us; an understanding that connects with other experiences of unitary reality I have presented throughout this study. It is that of the imagination, or to use Boehme's term: *Magia*.

> For it [wisdom] is that which is uttered, which the Father utters out of the center of the Heart by the Holy Spirit, and stands in divine forms and images, in the ocular view of the Holy Tri-unity of God. . . .It generates not the colors and figures which shine forth in it, and are revealed in the ground and essence; but all is together an eternal *Magia*, and dwells with the center of the heart in itself, and by the spirit goes forth from the center out of itself, and manifests itself in the eye of virgin wisdom endlessly. (1958, p. 9)

What is it that Boehme states is "all together an eternal *Magia*?" It is, first of all, a vital link between the human and the divine. If unitary reality or the *unus mundus* is the "place" of the connection, then the eternal *Magia* is a description of the process. And, as it is the very realm of the imaginal that we have been discussing—dreams, visions, illuminations, symbols—Boehme has in one statement on eternal *Magia* in the Godhead provided a nexus to it all. How else to understand our creation in the *image* of God, than as co-participants in the divine *imagi*-nation?

If we love because we are first loved by God, then perhaps we also imagine because we first are *imagined* by God. Boehme tells us that it is through the Divine Imagination that God has created the world.

> Having mirrored Himself in the Sophia, God "imagines" by projecting Himself into her, actualizes in finite forms the infinite richness of his creative potentiality. Then Sophia translates the divine Word into forms and colors.... Boehme tells how our universe, devastated since the fall, remains despite everything a mirror of Sophia and which, however troubled, aspires to incarnate her.... Thus, the universe, the distorted reflection of this archetypal and original mirror, tends to fulfill its model, its *Vorbild*, its Idea. (Faivre, 2000, pp. 138–39)

Faivre concludes this passage by reminding us that Boehme regards nothing to be a better symbolic representation of this Idea "than a beautiful meadow covered with flowers" (Ibid., p. 139). But if the created world/nature represents this "distorted reflection," so then can the soul. In *The Way to Christ*, Boehme refers to the soul as the bridegroom of Sophia, and in a beautiful passage reminiscent of *The Song of Songs*, has Sophia say,

> O noble bridegroom, keep your face before me and give me your fire-beams. Lead your desire into me,

and ignite me. By my meekness, I shall then change your fire-beams into a white-light, and direct my love through your fire-beams into your fire's essence and I shall kiss you eternally. (1978, p. 58)

We are presented images—sometimes when we most need them—images that lead us to where we can recognize the *unus mundus* and the divine. We are, each of us, enabled to hear the sound of deep calling to us and receive it in the deepest reaches of our inmost parts, *in intima mea.*

The experience of unitary reality is for us a kind of inheritance, but it is not an exclusive inheritance—something that is there for only the elect or the privileged few. It is our inheritance.

I have attempted, through all of the examples presented, to demonstrate how we get glimpses that this is a reality that is accessible to all. I have explored, in certain dreams and illuminations of Boehme and Jung and selected writings that emerged from them, something of the nature of the experience of unitary reality. I have also presented the examples of patients, one of whom had experienced that at "[t]he core is this nothingness. This *space* of nothing." Her encounter with the abyss needed to take place on several levels "in order for the nothing to become a something in which she could experience" through the transcendent function of the psyche "a presence." Another in-depth patient example revealed, after a long and troubling inner (and outer) journey, peopled with negative animus figures and torturers, the emergence of a powerful symbol of healing: a mandala wheel of her family on the circumference of a circle surrounding a burning fire in the center.

Finally, I believe that what is occurring in these experiences of unitary reality is a form of summoning, or, in a reference to the Psalms (42:7), a process of "deep calling unto deep." It is as if the Self were directing us, "whose souls thirst for the living God," to a deeper experience of life, to a level where the ego is not in control, but perhaps is perched on the limb of a tree staring into the void at the rising star of the self-same Self. If we are fortunate, we are able to incarnate this new experience, or are assisted in doing so through the presence in our lives of a holding place, such as the vessel or container of psychotherapy.

The encounter with unitary reality is a specific experience of otherness that involves passage through a fundamental dynamism or tension of the opposites. There appears to be a factor of stress, or suffering, again as in Psalm 42, "Why are you cast down, O my soul, and why are you disquieted within me?" This suffering catalyzes, or perhaps results from, the clashing of such opposites, to mount to this point of tension. The ego shifts away from a position of primacy by engaging with what is real and what is radically other. It is moved out of first place as the Self comes into consciousness.

In the end, we are not left with a nameless, meaningless chaos, some kind of grand "cosmic joke." In the experience of the abyss or of "the divine as eternity, truth and goodness," we come to see that we reflect a far deeper reality than our ego consciousness could possibly know. We may see through the "air hole" into the dark, preexistent void, but our longing gaze is met and returned by the light of a star.

It is there that we encounter the possibility of the *mysterium coniunctionis*, the passionate union of human and divine, the soul with Sophia, the image of the image. It is there that we are present "when deep calls unto deep."

In the words of the Magi (by way of T. S. Eliot),

> A cold coming we had of it,
> Just the worst time of the year
> For a journey, and such a long journey;
> The ways deep and the weather sharp,
> The very dead of winter. (Eliot, 1962, p. 69)

References

Agosin, T. (1992). "Psychosis, Dreams, and Mysticism in the Clinical Domain." In F. Halligan and J. Shea (eds.), *The Fires of Desire*. (pp. 41–65). New York: Crossroad.

Alleman, G. (1932). *A Critique of Some Philosophical Aspects of the Mysticism of Jacob Boehme*. Philadelphia: University of Pennsylvania.

Begley, S. (March 11, 2002). "The Schizophrenic Mind." *Newsweek*.

Berdyaev, N. (1935). *Freedom and Spirit* (O. Clarke, Trans.). New York: Scribner's.

———— (1936). *The Meaning of History* (G. Reavey, trans.). London: Geoffrey Bles.

———— (1946). *Spirit and Reality* (G. Reavey, trans.). London: Geoffrey Bles.

Blake, W. (1988). *Selected Poetry*. London: Penguin.

Boehme, J. (1911) *The Forty Questions of the Soul* (J. Sparrow, trans.). London: John M. Watkins.

———— (1915). *The Aurora* (J. Sparrow, trans.). London: John M. Watkins.

———— (1930). *On the Election of Grace* (J. R. Earle, trans.). London: Constable and Company, Ltd.

———— (1958). *Six Theosophic Points and Other Writings* (J. Earle, trans.). Ann Arbor: The University of Michigan Press.

———— (1965). *Mysterium Magnum* (Vols. 1–2) (J. Sparrow, trans.). London: John M. Watkins.

———— (1969). *The Signature of All Things*. Cambridge: James Clarke & Co., Ltd.

———— (1978). *The Way to Christ* (P. Erb, trans.). New York: Paulist.

———— (1991). *The Key of Jacob Boehme* (W. Law, trans). Grand Rapids, MI: Phanes Press.

Brooke, R. (1997). Correspondence: "Phenomenologists Reading Jung," *San Francisco Jung Institute Library Journal*, Vol. 15, no. 4, 67–71.

Brome, V. (1981). *Jung: Man and Myth*. New York: Atheneum.

Bromhall, W. (1955). *The Princess and the Woodcutter's Daughter*. New York: Knopf.

Cooper, J. C. (1987). *An Illustrated Encyclopaedia of Traditional Symbols*. (London; Thames and Hudson).

Cousins, E. H. (1990). The Self and Not-Self in Christian Mysticism. In R. Carter (ed.), *God, The Self and Nothingness*. (pp. 59–71). New York: Paragon.

———— (1992). *Christ of the 21st Century*. Rockport, MA: Element Books.

Edinger, E. (1995). *Melville's "Moby-Dick": An American Nekyia*. Toronto: Inner City Books.

———— (1996). *The New God-Image*. Wilmette, IL: Chiron.

Eliade, M. (1964). *Shamanism: Archaic Techniques of Ecstasy* (W. Trask, trans.). Princeton University Press.

Eliot, T. S. (1962). *"The Waste Land" and Other Poems*. New York: Harcourt, Brace and World.

Encyclopedia Americana (1959). New York: Americana Corporation.

Faivre, A. (2000). *Theosophy, Imagination, Tradition*. Albany: State University of New York Press.

Guntrip, H. (1968). *Schizoid Phenomena, Object Relations and the Self*. London: Hogarth.

Hazell, J. (1996). *H. J. S. Guntrip: A Psychoanalytical Biography*. London: Free Association Books.

Haughton, R. (1981). *The Passionate God*. New York: Paulist.

Harding, E. (1965). *The I and the Not I*. Princeton: Princeton University Press.

————. "The Value and Meaning of Depression." *Bulletin for the Analytical Psychology Club of New York* (1970), 1–15.

Heisig, J. (1972). "The VII Sermones: Play and Theory." *Spring*.

———— (1979). *Imago Dei*. Cranbury, NJ: Bucknell University Press.

Hoeller, S. (1982). *The Gnostic Jung and the Seven Sermons to the Dead*. Wheaton, ILL.: The Theosophical Publishing House.

Horne, M. (1998) "Review, *How Does the Transcendent Function?*" *San Francisco Jung Institute Library Journal*, vol. 17, no. 2, 21–42.

Jung, C. G. (1957). *Psychiatric Studies*. In H. Read, M. Fordham, G. Adler, & W. McGuire (eds.), CW 1. New York: Pantheon.

———— (1956). *Symbols of Transformation*. CW 5. Princeton University Press.

———— (1921). *Psychological Types*. CW 6. Princeton University Press.

———— (1966). *Two Essays on Analytical Psychology*. CW 7. Princeton University Press.

———— (1960). *The Structure and Dynamics of the Psyche*. CW 8. New York: Pantheon Books.

———— (1959a). *The Archetypes and the Collective Unconscious*. In CW 9.I. New York: Pantheon.

———— (1959b). *Aion*. CW 9.II. New York: Pantheon.

———— (1958). *Psychology and Religion: West and East*. CW 11. Princeton University Press.

———— (1968). *Psychology and Alchemy*. CW 12. Princeton University Press.

———— (1983). *Alchemical Studies*. CW 13. Princeton University Press.

———— (1989). *Mysterium Coniunctionis*. CW 14. Princeton University Press.

———— (1966). *The Spirit in Man, Art, and Literature*. CW 15. New York: Pantheon.

———— (1954) *The Symbolic Life*. CW 18. New York: Pantheon.

———— (1963). *Memories, Dreams, Reflections*. A. Jaffé (ed.). New York: Random House.

———— (1973). *Letters* (vol. 1), G. Adler (ed.). Princeton University Press.

———— (1975). *Letters* (vol. 2), G. Adler (ed.). Princeton University Press.

———— (1988). *Nietzsche's Zarathustra*, J. Jarrett (ed.). Princeton University Press.

Kalsched, D. (1996). *The Inner World of Trauma: Archetypal Defenses of the Personal Spirit*. London: Routlege.

Lesmeister, R. (1998). *"Zum Problem des Bösen in der postmodernen Realität,"* Unpublished lecture at XIV International Congress for Analytical Psychology.

Levinas, E. (1981). *Otherwise Than Being; or, Beyond Essence*. (A. Lingis, trans.). The Hague: Martinus Nijhoff.

———— (1969). *Totality and Infinity*. (A. Lingis, trans.). Pittsburgh: Duquesne University Press.

McLachlan, J. (1992). *The Desire to Be God*. New York: Peter Lang.

Madden, K. (1996). "Review, *Theology and Pastoral Counseling: A New Interdisciplinary Approach*, by Deborah Hunsinger," *Journal of Religion and Health* , winter, 361–64.

————. "The Dark Interval: Inner Transformation through Mourning and Memory." *Journal of Religion and Health: Psychology, Spirituality and Medicine,*, 36, no. 1 (spring, 1997): 29–51.

———— (Spring 2001) "From Speechlessness to Presence." *Journal of Religion and Health*. vol. 40, no. 1. 185–204.

————. "Images of the Abyss." *Journal of Religion and Health: Psychology, Spritituality and Medicine* 42, no. 2 (summer, 2003):117–31.

Martensen, H. (1949). *Jacob Boehme, Studies in His Life and Teaching*. (T. R. Evans, trans.). London: Rockliff.

McKelway, A. (1964). *The Systematic Theology of Paul Tillich*. New York: Delta.

Miller, J. (1993). *The Passion of Michael Foucault*. New York: Doubleday.

Neumann, E. (1954). "Mystical Man." In *Papers from the Eranos Yearbooks*. (R. Manheim and R. F. C. Hull, trans.) vol. 5. London.

———— (1989). *The Place of Creation*. Princeton University Press.

Palmer, M. (1997). *Freud and Jung on Religion*. London: Routledge.

Pannikar, R. (1989). *The Silence of God* (R. R. Barr, trans.). Maryknoll, NY: Orbis.

Olney, J. (1980). *The Rhizome and the Flower.* Berkeley: University of California Press.

Perry, J. W. (1999). *Trials of the Visionary Mind.* Albany: State University of New York Press.

———, Perry, J. W., and O'Callaghan, M. "Mental Breakdown as HealingExperience," *Global Vision Interviews* www.global-vision.org/dream, 1992, 1–13.

Quispel, G. (1968). "C. G. Jung and Gnosis: The *Septem Sermones ad Mortuous and Basilides.*" R. Segal (ed.), *The Gnostic* Jung. 219–38.

Ricœur, P. (1970). *Freud and Philosophy: An Essay on Interpretation* (D. Savage, trans.). Yale University Press.

——— (1980). "Toward a Hermeneutic of the Idea of Revelation," in his *Essays on Biblical Interpretation.* L. S. Mudge (ed.), Philadelphia: Fortress.

Romanyshyn, R. (2000). "Yes, Indeed! Do Call the World The Vale of Soul Making." D. Slattery and L. Corbett (eds.) *Depth Psychology: Meditations in the Field.* Carpinteria, CA: Daimon Verlag.

Rosenau, P. M. (1992). *Post-modernism and the Social Sciences: Insights, Inroads, and Intrusions.* Princeton University Press.

Samuels, A., Shorter, B. and Plaut, F. (1986). *A Critical Dictionary of Jungian Analysis.* New York: Routledge & Kegan Paul.

Schwartz-Salant, N. (1995). "On the Interactive Field as the Analytic Object." M. Stein (ed.). *The Interactive Field in Analysis.* Wilmette, IL: Chiron. 1–36.

——— and Stein, M. eds. (1988). *The Borderline Personality in Analysis.* Wilmette, IL: Chiron.

Segal, R. A. (1992). *The Gnostic Jung.* Princeton: PrincetonUniversityPress.

Sidoli, M. (1993). "When the Meaning Gets Lost in the Body: Psychosomatic Disturbances as a Failure of the Transcendent Function." *Journal of Analytical Psychology,* 39: 175–90.

Stoudt, J. J. (1957). *Sunrise to Eternity.* Philadelphia: University of Pennsylvania Press.

Tarnas, R. (1991). The Passion of the Western Mind: Understanding the Ideas that Have Shaped Our World View. New York: Random House.

Tougas, C. (1997). "*Correspondence: Phenomenologists Reading Jung,*" *San Francisco Jung Institute Library Journal,* vol. 15, no. 4, 71–75.

Tournier, P. (1954). *Journal of Psychotherapy as a Religious Process.* 1, 12–21.

Turner, V. (1967). *The Forest of Symbols.* Cornell University Press.

Ulanov, A. (1996). *The Functioning Transcendent*. Wilmette, IL: Chiron.

———— (1997). "Transference, the transcendent function and transcendence." *Journal of Analytical Psychology*, 42, 119–38.

———— (Fall 1999a). Countertransference and the Self. *Journal of Jungian Theory and Practice*, vol. 1, 5–26.

———— (1999b). *Religion and the Spiritual in Carl Jung*. Mahweh, NJ: Paulist.

Ulanov, B. (1973). Mysticism and Negative Presence. *The Journal of the Ancient Near Eastern Society of Columbia University*. vol. 5. 411–20.

———— (1983). *Prayers of St. Augustine*. Minneapolis: Seabury.

———— (1992). *Jung and the Outside World*. Wilmette: Chiron.

Versluis, A. (1999). *Wisdom's Children*. Albany: State University of New York Press.

von Franz, M-L. (1975). *C. G. Jung: His Myth in Our Time* (W. H. Kennedy, trans.). New York: G.P. Putnam's Sons.

———— (1997). *Archetypal Dimensions of the Psyche*. Boston: Shambhala.

Waite, A.E. (1940). *Three Famous Mystics*. Philadelphia: The David McKay Company.

Waterfield, R. (Ed.). (1989). *Jacob Boehme: Essential Readings*. Wellingborough, UK: Crucible.

Wehr, G. (1988). *Jung*. (D. M. Weeks, trans.). Boston: Shambala.

Winnicott, D. W. (1958). *Collected Papers: Through Paediatrics to Psychoanalysis*. London: Tavistock.

———— (1962). *The Maturational Process and the Facilitating Environment*. New York: International Universities Press.

Wood, D. K. (1982). "The Twentieth-century Revolt against Time: Belief and Becoming in the Thought of Berdyaev, Eliot, Huxley, and Jung." *The Secular Mind*. W. Wagar (ed.). New York: Holmes and Meier.

Wickes, F. (1950). *The Inner World of Man*. Boston: Sigo.

Young-Eisendrath, P. (1996). *The Gifts of Suffering: Finding Insight, Compassion, and Renewal*. Reading, MA: Addison-Wesley.

———— and Hall, J. (1991). *Jung's Self Psychology: A Constructivist Perspective*. New York: Guilford Press.

———— and Dawson, T. (1997). *The Cambridge Companion to Jung*. Cambridge: Cambridge University Press.